Receive
YE ONE ANOTHER

Receive
YE ONE ANOTHER

**Taking Temple Marriage
the Second Mile**

Larry W. Lewis

CFI
Springville, Utah

ISBN 13: 978-1-55517-911-3
ISBN 10: 1-55517-911-8

Published by CFI, an imprint of Cedar Fort, Inc., 925 N. Main, Springville, UT, 84663
Distributed by Cedar Fort, Inc. www.cedarfort.com

The Library of Congress cataloged the 2006 edition of this book as follows:

Lewis, Larry W.
  Receive ye one another : taking temple marriage the second mile /
by Larry W. Lewis.
    p. cm.
  Includes bibliographical references.
  ISBN 1-55517-911-8 (pbk. : alk. paper)
  1. Marriage--Religious aspects--Church of Jesus Christ of Latter-Day Saints.
  2. Marriage--Religious aspects--Mormon Church. 3. Church of Jesus Christ of Latter-day Saints--Doctrines. 4. Mormon Church--Doctrines. I. Title.

  BX8641.L49 2006
  248.8'44088289332--dc22

                                                            2006013645

Cover design by Adam Riggs
Cover design © 2006 by Lyle Mortimer
Printed in the United States of America

10 9 8 7 6 5 4 3 2

Printed on acid-free paper

DEDICATION

To Kendell—for the joy of her company.

CONTENTS

And now, as the preaching of the word had a great ten-
dency to lead the people to do that which was just—yea, it
had had more powerful effect upon the minds of the people
than the sword, or anything else, which had happened unto
them—therefore Alma thought it was expedient that they
should try the virtue of the word of God.

—Alma 31:5

PREFACE

I am a clinical therapist who works predominantly with active members of The Church of Jesus Christ of Latter-day Saints. The majority of the couples I work with have temple marriages. As might be expected, most of the men and women who request my services have marriages that are under stress. Some of them are considering divorce.

I've had much opportunity to compare temple marriages with civil marriages. There are marked differences between the two types of marriage, although not all Church members could explain what these differences are. I'm convinced that many advantages of a temple marriage are realized in *this life*. The promise of being together forever gives us hope for the future, but healing our wounded hearts is often what we need right now.

Temple covenants with the Lord are quite different from the vows that men and women exchange in a civil marriage. We can't conduct our marriages on the principles of a civil marriage and realize the blessings of a temple marriage. It's only possible to obtain covenant blessings by following covenant principles. It's therefore essential that we know what those principles are.

A marriage counselor who doesn't know those principles can only go so far in helping a couple realize a successful temple marriage. There is great value in teaching married partners to communicate, to compromise, and to share control. But what can be done when what is called for is a complete change of heart? Sometimes the heart has to be sent back to the factory for repairs. That is when a counselor must know the principles of a temple marriage.

The most exhilarating moment in my professional career is when a client suddenly catches on that the gospel applies to his life *literally*. There is often the terrifying realization that the Lord is guiding him along a path where his *only* chance is a miracle! The scriptures take on new meaning at such times. I've been privileged to witness many such moments. It's my hope that this book will help LDS couples, particularly temple-married couples, to experience these insights and realize these blessings.

Throughout the book, I have referred to specific techniques or assignments as guardrails. I do this to emphasize that the prerequisite condition is a broken heart and a contrite spirit. Once a client's heart has changed, once he *desires* to be Christlike, then all that's left is to bring his behavior into line with his spirit. A driver who already wants to stay on the highway requires only a guardrail at the curves and cliffs.

Another underlying premise is that we only realize the blessings we ask for. Almost everyone enters counseling asking what I call justice questions. They ask, "Is it fair that I should have to put up with this circumstance?" or "Shouldn't my partner do things differently?" or "What am I willing to settle for?" I consider the primary art of counseling to be helping the client shift to asking mercy questions. Healing miracles follow when clients begin to ask, "What does the Lord want me to do?" or "Where do I find the strength to bless my spouse?" or "What would constitute a blessing in my partner's life?" I invite the reader to watch for this shift from justice questions to mercy questions in each example in this book.

The examples I've used are taken from real life. However, to preserve the privacy of my clients, I've combined the stories of different people who had related experiences. All clinical cases mentioned in this book were disguised in this manner to maintain confidentiality. I used fictitious names solely for convenience in recounting these familiar composite stories.

With regard to my own personal experiences, I tried to be as strictly accurate as my memory permits. I'm deeply grateful to my wife and children for allowing me to share some of our personal moments in this book. Kendell seems resolved that this is one of the hazards of my trade. Additionally, I related a few experiences of personal friends, with their permission.

I am also grateful to Dr. A. Dean Byrd, a friend and colleague, who spent many hours reviewing the initial manuscript and whose many corrections and suggestions are reflected in the final work. Finally, I'm thankful that my publisher was willing to devote the extra time that beginning authors require, and that my editor provided the much-needed polishing.

This book reflects only my *personal* perspective on the gospel of Jesus Christ. I'm not a spokesman for The Church of Jesus Christ of Latter-day Saints or any of its leaders. If anything here seems to contradict what our prophets have taught, then I'm wrong. I can live with that.

And Adam said, This is now bone of my bones, and flesh of my flesh: she shall be called Woman, because she was taken out of Man. Therefore shall a man leave his father and his mother, and shall cleave unto his wife: and they shall be one flesh.

—Genesis 2:23–24

Chapter One
BONE OF MY BONES

When Adam met Eve in the Garden of Eden, he recognized immediately how special she would be among all that God had created. All the other delightful creations—rock and water, plant and animal—were optional. With every mountain or stream, orchid or parakeet, each might have been created differently or been replaced by something else. An inexhaustible variety in nature testifies that there is no single arrangement to flowers, feathers, or fur.

But with the introduction of his wife, Adam realized that here at last could be another—not himself, yet like himself. The two of them would be able to accept and receive each other as the first married couple. The Lord had brought Eve to Adam because "it is not good that the man should be alone; I will make him an help meet for him" (Genesis 2:18). The word *meet* suggests that they were a matched set, that notwithstanding the many differences in appearance and temperament between them, they were still so fundamentally alike that Adam could call them "one flesh" (Genesis 2:23). It was obvious that they were meant to stay together.

How they must have loved each other! Of all that had been created, only the two of them could appreciate the world in quite the same way. Only they could share *human* feelings as they watched the sun set and the stars appear, the wind rustling the leaves on the tree of life, or the subtle differences in how the two of them walked or smiled. Small wonder that Adam could not bear to be separated from Eve after she had partaken of the forbidden fruit but rather joined her in mortality. Having received one another, they were never to be parted for eternity.

There is, however, no guarantee that all couples are going to feel that way. Many married couples have become emotionally *estranged,* which is the opposite of being "one flesh." To be estranged is to lack a sense of kinship, to lose the awareness that you are made of the same stuff. Without such feelings, Adam might have hesitated before sharing his deeper feelings with Eve, afraid she might receive their similarities yet reject their differences. Without such an awareness, Eve might have made plans for her day with no sense of how Adam would fit into those plans. Moreover, both might have been tempted to seek that oneness with someone else (had there been anyone else).

Marriage has both pleasant and practical features, but it is a couple's perception of union that lends meaning to all else. The word *love* is used in so many different ways that it's not an easy word to define, yet when Adam declared that he and Eve were "one flesh," he may have grasped love's deepest meaning.

HOW WE LEARN TO LOVE

Adam and Eve loved each other, and from that love came children. Did those children also come into the world with a need to be received by someone else? How did they learn to love? Long before these children married, it was with Adam and Eve, their parents, that they first felt made out of the same stuff. As the children were born, their parents and siblings made room for them in their hearts, and they were received as *family*.

That sense of relatedness has a powerful effect upon the hearts of new parents. They seem to actually enjoy the untidy kisses of their babies. They recognize their child's cry from all others in the nursery, and they quickly respond. Furthermore, when caring for their children, parents are not always on their best behavior. Children aren't company, they're *family*—right off the bat!

Even within the first few weeks of life, an infant can tell if there is a change of caregivers. I've witnessed that it generally takes a few days for an adopted baby to adjust to his new family, until once again "this is now bone of my bones" (Genesis 2:23). We take this attachment process for granted, but it is a monumental achievement for a child to identify kin and to feel it so fundamentally that he is prepared for the next step, the individuation process lovingly referred to as the terrible twos.

The toddler who loudly announces, "*I do it, Mommy!*" is actually testifying through his rebellion that he has developed an emotional foundation. He can only push his mother away because he knows she isn't going to go away but will remain as his emotional reference point. A child will survive a missed meal or an irritable parent now and again, but an infant who does not have parents who receive him as their own is like a blind person wandering in a room so large he cannot find the wall. There is nothing to push away from. Such children are willful, not rebellious; they ignore laws, not break them. Whether the failure to attach is inborn or acquired, such a child is significantly handicapped early on and frequently remains so into adulthood. From the inception of our lives, we need to belong to someone, to be received as kin—not because we measure up but because someone chooses to receive us.

When my youngest son was a toddler, we always knew

when he wanted to be picked up. He would not say a word but would raise both arms over his head and look longingly at us. If we didn't respond immediately, he would raise his arms a little higher, and a look of urgency would come into his eyes. If for any reason that didn't work, he would stamp his feet and whine and renew his reach toward heaven. Eventually, his mother or I would put down what we were doing and lift him into our arms, and his desperation would turn to a snugly peaceful feeling. Our son had no words for what he wanted so much, but the scriptures call it being received.

I believe that receiving is the key to growing up emotionally and spiritually. When our lives include being received and receiving others, we find that we are bigger than our challenges, temptations, and fears—and that translates to how much joy and success we experience in being alive. Conversely, of course, when receiving isn't happening in our lives, we find ourselves to be smaller than our challenges, temptations, and fears. This one principle explains why one person is able to climb out of life's sand traps, while another person is helpless to do so.

As we grow older, we take the next step toward marriage when we establish a sort of *supplemental kinship* with a network of friends. We identify a crowd, our kind of people who wear similar fashions, play similar games, listen to similar music, and use similar slang phrases. If we are successful in getting others to accept us as card-carrying members of the crowd, we can then develop a closer, better-defined clique with others of that crowd. Our clique can serve many functions of a family, providing us the comparisons we need to further define ourselves as individuals. Then, if we are reasonably successful in joining a crowd and forming a clique, the next step is to form one best friendship. For many of us, the defining moment of adolescence occurs when we can say, "My friend and I have received each other as best friends. It is so, and we both know it."

It was heartwarming several years ago when my then eleven-year-old daughter introduced me to her new best friend. She was thrilled by how much they were alike and how much they had in common. After a few weeks, she was equally thrilled by how different they were, as they divided up the turf of who was better at singing and who was better at skating, who had prettier eyes and who had prettier hair, who made better grades and who was more popular. Together, they could do anything; individually, they were only half a team. They learned about loyalty in their new dyad and even a little about the pain of disloyalty. They were successful in forming a secure friendship, and they began to use it as a launch platform to form relationships with boys. They would watch boys and decide whom they liked, but of course that part of life was still very much in the future. What counted at the moment was their best friend, the one person who truly *understood.*

And then comes the day when friendships fade in comparison to a new kind of relationship. I enjoy watching how young couples fall in love. It's as though they each spend their childhood sketching out an image of the perfect spouse on a transparent template, and then they compare every likely candidate to that template. When there is a near match, they experience the euphoric sense of discovery we call infatuation. *Where have you been all my life?* With true love, though, the template itself changes, gradually conforming to the image of the loved one. *I find now that I'm only attracted to people who remind me of you.*

Brian and Marci

As a junior in college, Marci was already frustrated with dating. She knew how to be pleasant and interesting, but she wasn't interested in any of the boys who responded to her smile. On the other hand, she envisioned the man of her dreams as confident, considerate, and devoted, yet also spontaneous and entertaining—someone like her father, perhaps, yet of course more youthful. Marci wasn't ready yet to trade in the freedom of her college days, but she knew the day would come when closeness would be more important to her than freedom. She wondered if her future husband was out there. Her roommate, Judy, cheerfully suggested that perhaps he had died in the Civil War, and she wouldn't meet him until the next life. Marci replied that her eternal mate had probably perished in the War in Heaven!

Marci was aware that a boy named Brian had dated Judy a couple of times, yet there didn't seem to be any chemistry between them. Still, Marci hoped to meet Brian someday, just so she'd know whom Judy was talking about. When they did meet, it was interest at first sight. Brian was both shorter and lighter complected than Marci had imagined her ideal sweetheart to be, but his smile and personality hit all the right buttons. Marci found she liked herself more when she was around Brian, and she felt natural being herself. They had dated for several weeks before it became obvious that neither of them was interested in dating anyone else.

A few months into the relationship, however, Marci began to experience a sense of disappointment. She noticed that Brian was less attentive when he was worried about a big test, and his sense of humor around his guy friends didn't seem so funny. Marci became less sure that Brian was her final answer. She realized that she was again scanning about for her dream companion.

Fortunately, neither of them was so impatient for marriage as to leap into an engagement. They continued dating for another year, and gradually Marci began to realize that she had *received* Brian into her life. Her heart swelled with the recognition of who he was, instead of merely how much he resembled her dreams. Her infatuation had turned into love.

Being young, Marci, at times, still tried to change Brian to match her template, not yet realizing how much she would miss him if she really had the power to turn him into someone else—which, of course, she didn't. That particular element of maturity would come a few years later. For now, they were in love and looking toward a temple marriage, when they would covenant with God to forever receive each other.

And so it is with each child, growing toward the day when he will "leave his father and his mother" (and his best friend, mission companion, and old girlfriend) and "cleave unto his wife: and they shall be one flesh" (Genesis 2:24). In this instance, the word *cleave* means something like splice or graft, implying a bond as fundamental as that between a newborn child and his parents. If both partners are emotionally ready for marriage, this bond can grow to be for life, natural and unforced, wholly received by each other as they were by their parents. For most of us, the story of our childhood culminates in what we hope will be such a marriage. Being so received is why we marry in the first place.

We have an inborn need to be received in all our most important relationships. Moreover, it's crucial that we are received as . . . It's not enough that my parents receive me as a cute kid; I want them to receive me as their son. I want to be more than one of Johnny's buddies; I want him to receive me as his best friend. I'm not satisfied when the girl I've been dating agrees to just be friends; I want her to receive me as her boyfriend. And it will never be enough for my wife to receive me as anything less than her eternal companion in the new and everlasting covenant.

"BECAUSE HE FIRST LOVED US"

Why is it so important for people to form permanent bonds with others? Some suppose that this is a genetically inborn need, since human babies are dependent for so long. This may be true, but perhaps a deeper truth was expressed in 1 John 4:19: "We love him, because he first loved us." Our spirits guard the memory that we once lived with Heavenly Father as His children. As Paul said, "The Spirit itself beareth witness with our spirit, that we are the children of God" (Romans 8:16).

In premortal life, we knew what it felt like to be unconditionally loved by the source of light and life; consequently, we have a hunger to return to His presence and be received by Him. Our LDS temple endowment presents us with a clear vision of how we should live in order to be received back into the presence of God. Don't we all yearn to knock on heaven's door and be received home? It is part of the Lord's plan of happiness that we attain this deepest desire, which is why so many scriptures address how we may be received by God:

> Therefore, whoso repenteth and cometh unto me as a little child, him will I receive. (3 Nephi 9:22)
>
> And whoso shall receive one such little child in my name receiveth me. (Matthew 18:5)
>
> He that receiveth you receiveth me, and he that receiveth me receiveth him that sent me. (Matthew 10:40)
>
> Go thy way unto thy brother, and first be reconciled to thy brother, and then come unto me with full purpose of heart, and I will receive you. (3 Nephi 12:24)
>
> His Lord said unto him, Well done, thou good and faithful servant: thou hast been faithful over a few things, I will make thee ruler over many things: enter thou into the joy of thy lord. (Matthew 25:21)

I believe that anyone brought back into God's presence would be instantly filled with overpowering feelings of love and a longing to be received by Him. This is exactly what happened when Jesus visited the Nephites at the temple in Bountiful:

> And it came to pass that the multitude went forth, and thrust their hands into his side, and did feel the prints of the nails in his hands and in his feet; and this they did do, going forth one by one until they had all gone forth. . . . And when they had all gone forth and had witnessed for themselves, they did cry out with one accord, saying: Hosanna! Blessed be the name of the Most High God! And they did fall down at the feet of Jesus, and did worship him. . . . And Nephi arose and went forth, and bowed himself before the Lord and did kiss his feet. (3 Nephi 11:15–19)

How many of us have wept when reading such scriptures, suddenly filled with a yearning to be back home again?

OBSTACLES ON THE PATH HOME

There is, however, something within that causes us to shy away from such a reunion. If we are spiritually sensitive, we are aware of the immense difference between our pale glory and the glory that Jesus now possesses. We want to embrace Him, but we know we would perish instantly if we were exposed to His glory. So we settle for an embrace and a whisper through the veil. The veil is not there simply to make us forget our premortal life; it shields and protects mortals from the glory of God.

Unless we are given some other form of protection, the veil must always be thick enough to protect us. And a veil that thick

is going to muffle our experience of everything on the other side, even our premortal memories. However, when we live our lives in accordance with the gospel of Jesus Christ, the veil can become less opaque to us. Those who can sustain the presence of the Spirit in their lives can also tolerate a thinner veil. But thin or thick, the veil must be there. It is frustrating to have something intervening between us and God, but we must remember that it is the veil that makes communion with Him possible at all.

Another significant barrier between ourselves and God is the guilt we feel because of our sins. Sometimes we transgress God's laws because we don't know it's sin. More often, however, we sin through choice; the veil prevents us from actually seeing Him, and we act as though He weren't watching us. The fact is, we are as likely to be childish, willful or rebellious, as we are to be child-like, trusting, and teachable. Each of us who has reached the age of accountability has sinned. While many of us sincerely seek a life free of sin, it isn't likely that we'll attain that goal in mortality. Hopefully, our batting average is improving, but most of us continue to sin from time to time.

The good news of the gospel is that there is no insurmountable barrier between us and God. As Paul said:

> For I am persuaded, that neither death, nor life, nor angels, nor principalities, nor powers, nor things present, nor things to come, nor height nor depth, nor any other creature, shall be able to separate us from the love of God, which is in Christ Jesus our Lord. (Romans 8:38–39)

We will not be forever separated from God. The atonement of Jesus Christ has made it possible for our sins to be forgiven and for us to eventually overcome sin altogether. There is a way back home.

One of the most comforting of the Lord's parables is *The Parable of the Prodigal Son*. The young man returned to his father's house after squandering his inheritance in riotous living, knowing he had lost any right to be received as a son but hoping he would be accepted there as a servant. The heart of this story is the father's reaction when his son appears:

> But when he was yet a great way off, his father saw him, and had compassion, and ran, and fell on his neck, and kissed him. And the son said unto him, Father, I have sinned against heaven, and in thy sight, and am no more worthy to be called thy son. But the father said to his servants, Bring forth the best robe, and put it on him; and put a ring on his hand, and shoes on his feet: And bring hither the fatted calf, and kill it; and let us eat, and be merry; For this my son was dead, and is alive again; he was lost, and is found. (Luke 15:20–24)

While the young man had indeed wasted away his inheritance, there was nothing to prevent his father from giving him unmerited gifts simply because he loved him. Thus it may be with each of us if we truly repent. There will certainly be consequences for our sins, but Christ will not turn His back on one of His repentant children. He has promised us that we can repent and come unto Him with a valid hope that He will receive us.

At the conclusion of the first day of the Lord's visit to the Nephites, He said to those who had come forth and felt the prints of the nails in His hands and in His feet, "And ye see that I have commanded that none of you should go away, but rather have commanded that ye should come unto me that ye might feel and see" (3 Nephi 18:25).

We may have confidence in the Lord's promises because we get a taste of them in this life. We hear God's voice as a whisper through the veil, and He sends signs and miracles to us from time to time. But most of the hugs we get come through other people. They come from our parents, siblings, children, other relatives, and from friends. And the hugs that most remind us of heaven are the hugs we receive from our spouses.

A UNIVERSAL NEED

We yearn to be received in our marriages as Adam received Eve. Adam could no more separate Eve from his life than he could separate his right hand from his wrist. There were no conditions, no *ifs*. If you treat me right, then I will receive you; if you mind yourself and stay in the Garden of Eden, then I will stick by you. Moreover, there were no *untils* either. I will receive you as my wife until we both grow up, until God creates another woman, or even until death do us part.

If this need to be received by God, family, and spouse is so universal, why is it that not all of us feel received in our marriages? Many couples have replaced appreciation and compassion with criticism and rejection, the very opposite of receiving one another. They often can conceive of no worse hell than being together forever. Others seem stingy with their love, as if afraid they'll run out if they love one person too much. Still others fear to enter into a marriage in the first place.

Thomas and Vicki

For example, Thomas was pressured into counseling by his mother, who just couldn't understand why her thirty-two-year-old son seemed so contentedly single. She worried that her own example of a temple marriage had somehow been lacking for him, and she wondered if Thomas had experienced a heartbreak he'd never shared with her, or if he had some secret fear of failure he couldn't talk about. She prayed for him to find the right girl,

11

and she also prayed that Heavenly Father would bless Thomas's future wife to be patient. Why didn't Thomas seem more anxious to be married? Wasn't he lonely?

In our first session, Thomas told me he had dated extensively and that more than once he had really considered marriage. Thomas conceded that he wished he were already married, but it was the *engagement thing* that was hard for him. Every time he seriously considered someone as a possible marriage partner, he'd compare his feelings for her with previous infatuations. Each time, he concluded that if he was able to leave her and keep shopping, then she must not be the right one. He wondered if he was even capable of true love.

As Thomas grew older, so did the young women he dated; fewer of them were willing to take the chance of growing attached, only to have him leave them in the end. Thomas hadn't realized the cause for his drop in popularity; he thought it was his receding hairline! As we discussed his past dating history, however, he became increasingly able to see things through others' eyes. He recognized that he'd raised the hopes of several of the girls he'd dated, only to leave them wondering what was wrong with themselves.

He'd assumed that if his own feelings were shallow, then no doubt so were his girlfriends' feelings. But as we discussed how most people wait for signs of reciprocal caring before they show their feelings, Thomas began to regret his unkindness. He wondered if he should stop dating altogether.

It was about this time that Vicki moved back into Thomas's stake. Thomas knew he was attracted to her, but he was careful to keep things on a friendship level, fearful of hurting her if it didn't work out. Sure enough, a few weeks later Thomas concluded that he should probably move on, since once again he took his ability to end a relationship as proof that he should. I asked him how he would know the real thing if he ever found it, and Thomas admitted he didn't know.

I shared with him the advice of my stake patriarch, that our prayer to Heavenly Father should not be, "Is this the girl Thou wouldst have me marry? If Thou wilt command me to do so, I will do it." Rather, we should pray, "If Thou wilt allow me to marry this girl, I covenant with Thee that I will do everything in my power to make her happy! May I take her to Thy temple?"

This was a new concept for Thomas. He had never considered that the sign he'd been seeking was not some overwhelming surge of infatuation but rather an undeniable desire to make her happy! Thomas told me that the high point of his dating experiences had always been when his girlfriends had seemed genuinely happy, and he had always wanted to prolong those moments. He'd never realized that this had been his payoff for dating all along!

Thomas wasn't sure that Vicki was "the one," but he looked forward to making their next date special for her. Perhaps this was the sign he had sought so long. He would know who to marry not by how excited he was to be with her but by how wonderful he felt when she was happy.

Thomas was never the confirmed bachelor everyone took him to be. He had always yearned for an eternal companionship, but fear of making the wrong choice had kept his dream out of reach. I wasn't too surprised when I received an invitation from Thomas and Vicki inviting me to their temple wedding six months later.

How can we ensure that temple marriages are going to succeed? Other than being sealed in the house of the Lord, is there something else we should do through the years that will transform our temple sealing into an eternal marriage? What is the connection between being sealed and being exalted together in the celestial kingdom?

As a family therapist, I have seen many couples who seem near to being "one flesh." Not all these men and women have been sealed in the temple, and many are not members of The Church of Jesus Christ of Latter-day Saints. There have always been those who seek a better way, who have discovered some eternal principles through their own experience. But though they may not have learned these eternal truths in the temple, they only achieve happiness to the degree that they apply the principles that are taught there. Moreover, as we will see in coming chapters, the most profound union is only possible for those couples who can share with each other their covenant relationship with the Lord.

So what about Latter-day Saint couples? Most of our own young couples prepare for their temple sealings by living the Lord's commandments, studying the scriptures, and being faithful in their church callings. Such efforts are very effective in preparing someone to receive his or her own temple endowment. Quite often, however, this is not adequate preparation for the temple sealing itself. On the day of their temple sealings, not many of our young grooms and brides can explain in their own words the covenant they are about to enter. We expect them to grow in their understanding of these sacred things—and rightly so. Yet perhaps if we helped them to better understand their temple covenants ahead of time, we might see more temple marriages grow into eternal marriages.

When a man and a woman are sealed in the temple, they want to be received by each other as they once wanted their parents to receive them and as they will always want the Lord to receive them. Just as the plan of happiness provides the way to overcome obstacles between us and the Lord, it also provides the way to overcome obstacles to our receiving one another in our marriages. For every challenge to a righteous temple marriage, there is a solution and a cure. In this world or the next, we will all someday realize that keeping our covenants is the only way to attain our heart's desire.

In the chapters ahead, we will examine how the doctrines of the restored gospel can transform our marriages. It is my hope that more of us will incorporate these principles into our hearts and our homes, and that temple marriage will continue to mean something different and wonderful to Latter-day Saints.

In the celestial glory there are three heavens or degrees; and in order to obtain the highest, a man must enter into this order of the Priesthood [meaning the new and everlasting covenant of marriage]; and if he does not, he cannot obtain it. He may enter into the other, but that is the end of his kingdom; he cannot have an increase.

—D&C 131:1–4

CHAPTER TWO

THE NEW AND EVERLASTING COVENANT

Latter-day Saints make sacred covenants through three ordinances: baptism, the temple endowment, and the temple sealing covenant. We know the doorway to the lowest degree of the celestial kingdom is baptism, and we just now read that the doorway into the highest degree of the celestial kingdom is the sealing of spouses (what we most often refer to as temple marriage). We are not told whether the middle degree of the celestial kingdom is attained by keeping the promises we make when we are endowed, but that seems to be a fair conclusion.

We don't fully comprehend how these degrees of celestial glory differ from one another, but we do know that in the highest degree of glory we will experience the illumination and happiness that our Heavenly Father enjoys. We also know that by making and keeping our covenants, we will more closely approximate the type of life that Heavenly Father lives. However, it is obvious that we must first know what we are promising before we can live by those promises. Before we can explore the temple sealing covenant, it is first necessary to understand the covenants we make at baptism and the temple endowment.

BAPTISM

I became a member of the Church in the late '60s when many young people were asking that great question, "Why?" (and also, "Why not?"). As I look back, I wish my own search for the truth had been more organized, but my search was genuine and deeply felt. I had no belief in a personal God and no confidence at all in organized religion. But I also knew that I lacked a star to steer by. Sometimes I became so aware that I was adrift in life that it was frightening, and I would call out (to the sky?). Sometimes I would cry.

One day, with no advance warning, the sky answered back. Literally in an instant, I became aware that a personal God was telling me to learn about Christianity from the Mormons. Because I did know a few Latter-day Saints, I was able to contact them as I had been directed. I took the missionary lessons during the next two weeks and was thrilled as the Mormon elders gave me the answers to so many of my questions about revelation, eternal progression, and the nature of Zion. I never doubted Joseph Smith's prophetic calling, the Book of Mormon, or (to everyone's surprise) the Word of Wisdom. However, I just couldn't relate to the doctrine of Christ or the Atonement. This was because my new relationship with God was too shallow to be affected much by my own sins. I was not yet repentant.

Toward the end of that instructional period, I felt directed to be baptized. I knew I was promising to live the commandments, but I hoped that somehow there might be some provision for only partial compliance. I wasn't overly confident in my ability to keep all of the commandments. I only knew that Heavenly Father wanted me to be baptized, and He didn't want me to postpone my baptism. To some extent, it felt as though it was His decision and not altogether mine.

The morning following my baptism, I awoke shortly after 6 A.M. with a strong awareness that the missionaries were visiting my home again. I hastened to dress, but then I began to wonder why they would be making calls so early in the morning. I suddenly realized that what I was sensing was the companionship of the Holy Ghost. Until then, I hadn't been able to identify what the presence of the Holy Ghost felt like. At that moment, however, I realized it was simply the feeling I always experienced whenever the missionaries visited me.

Like those reading this book, I have sinned since my baptism. It was nearly a year after my baptism that I really repented in earnest. I felt shame and remorse for my sins, and I began to perceive the immense distance between myself and my Heavenly Father. Like Alma in the Book of Mormon, I wanted to "become extinct both soul and body, that I might not be brought to stand in the presence of my God, to be judged of my deeds" (Alma 36:15).

Actually, the Book of Mormon was my lifeline to hope in those days. Through its pages, I finally came to know the role of Jesus Christ and His atonement in my life. I came to experience the joy that we feel when our Savior tells us "thy sins are forgiven thee, and thou shalt be blessed" (Enos 1:5).

But being mortal, I sinned again, and once again had to ask myself, "What is wrong with me that I can know the truth with a sure knowledge, and yet sometimes I just don't care whether it's true or not?" It was Moroni's closing testimony on the last page of the Book of Mormon that finally gave me the answer to my question:

> And if ye shall deny yourselves of all ungodliness,
> and love God with all your might, mind and strength,
> then is his grace sufficient for you, that by his grace
> ye may be perfect in Christ. (Moroni 10:32)

Just as the Spirit led me by the hand when I made the decision to be baptized, I will need to be led by the hand for the rest of my life. I feel as though I'm walking down icy stairs and need to grasp the railing with both hands. Trying to keep my own balance as I carefully descend the steps is never going to be enough for me; I dare not let go of the railing. I don't expect to reach the point in mortality where I can be perfect just because of what I know to be true. My only hope is to be *perfect in Christ*, relying on His grace from moment to moment.

At first, I was trying to develop holiness through willpower alone. I must have been thinking, *As soon as the desires of my heart become entirely right, I'm going to present myself to my Savior for His approval.* I must have been crazy! I might as well have been an unplugged lamp, striving to shine so brightly on my own that I would merit electricity.

As Nephi says so simply, "For we labor diligently to write, to persuade our children, and also our brethren, to believe in Christ, and to be reconciled to God; for we know that it is by grace that we are saved, after all we can do" (2 Nephi 25:23). In fighting temptation, "all we can do" isn't very much. Yet, when I lean upon the Savior and call on Him to help me keep the Holy Spirit in my life, my temptations shrink, often to such a degree that I can overcome them with something as weak and fragile as my willpower. I can feel the difference, and it is very real.

As I look back, my baptism was more than a ceremony to mark my entrance into the true church. It was a covenant with my Savior that as I pray, study, serve, sacrifice, and keep the commandments, the companionship of the Holy Spirit will begin to change me. The covenant of baptism is to *live as Jesus lives* by keeping the Holy Spirit present with us. The Lord's half of the covenant is to provide what we ourselves lack—the power to keep the commandments.

THE TEMPLE ENDOWMENT

Baptism is an ordinance of the Aaronic Priesthood. This is quite natural since this priesthood holds the keys to "the gospel of repentance" (D&C 13). The temple endowment, on the other hand, is an ordinance of the Melchizedek Priesthood, which holds the keys of "all the spiritual blessings of the church" (D&C 107:18), and therefore makes manifest the presence and power of God.

The first mention of the endowment in the scriptures is the direction Jesus gave to his apostles that they should remain in Jerusalem until they should be "endued with power from on high" (Luke 24:49). It is significant that the promise was of an investiture of power. The apostles had already received the Melchizedek Priesthood, but now they were going to receive the knowledge that would enable them to fully use it.

Latter-day Saints rightly hesitate before discussing in any detail the covenants we make in the temple, because some things are so sacred that we only talk about them when we're inside the temple itself. Therefore, I'm going to keep my discussion of temple covenants fairly general and will not be quoting directly from either the endowment or the sealing ceremonies.

In the endowment, we learn how Heavenly Father organizes His affairs both in heaven and on earth, and we see how we fit into that organization. We learn to call upon Him, to make a place for Him in our lives, and to seek the gifts and power of the Holy Ghost. We also learn the proper role of marriage in our lives. Finally, we learn how much the Lord requires of those who would build His kingdom in the latter days.

In addition to instruction and covenant making, there are other elements in the temple endowment that are symbolic. Not only are these symbols used to teach doctrines and ordinances, but they are also evidences that covenants were made. In like manner, the ring on my left hand is not my marriage, but its presence is a witness to all that I am married. It is symbolic proof that an ordinance occurred. It would be even more so if such symbols as rings could *only* be obtained by getting married, as are the symbols of the temple.

With such symbols to help remember the covenants they make in their temple endowment, young men and women are prepared to go forth as missionaries. Despite their youth, relative lack of formal education, and minimal supervision, these elders and sisters perform *miracles* in their missionary service! Mature men and women often yield to the Spirit these young missionaries bring into their home (just as I did) and experience remarkable conversions! Through repentance and the power of the Holy Spirit, even dysfunctional families can find healing and forgiveness, and in only a few years, they can be found kneeling in a temple to be sealed together for time and all eternity.

The Lord honors these young people in the most remarkable ways. The average elder or sister missionary can expect to witness healings, the gift of tongues, miraculous protections, or rebuking of evil spirits. During my mission, I recall once giving a priesthood administration to a child with a burning temperature and feeling his head become cool beneath our hands. On another occasion, I watched a companion's fumbling command of the Spanish language suddenly transform into beautiful fluency as he testified of the Savior's atonement. These extraordinary events may seem like stories out of scripture, but most missionaries enjoy such experiences during their missions.

A few years ago, a very close friend was embarrassed during fast and testimony meeting as person after person came to the stand to testify how the Lord had blessed their lives through his home teaching visits. Most of this service consisted of encouragement, spiritual comfort, or priesthood blessings. I could recall many times when he had lifted me spiritually in just such ways. Another member of the ward finally came forth and testified that even though this brother was not his home teacher, he still had a testimony of the restored gospel anyway. Everyone laughed, but the thought lingered in our minds that home teaching could be something pretty special if we put our faith in it. My friend had kept the promises he made in his temple endowment, and that had made the difference.

Those who have been baptized can seek a greater level of discipleship by receiving their own endowments. At the close of His mortal ministry, Jesus held a Passover meal with His disciples, and He told them, "He that believeth on me, the works that I do shall he do also; and greater works than these shall he do" (John 14:12). But this level of discipleship comes with a price. Jesus had previously taught them, "So likewise, whosoever he be of you that forsaketh not all that he hath, he cannot be my disciple" (Luke 14:33). He also told them of persecution: "The time cometh, that whosoever killeth you will think that he doeth God service" (John 16:2).

We may wonder if we would have proven faithful had we been called to be the Lord's disciples. Those who receive their temple endowments are in fact committing to be disciples, for they are covenanting to *work as Jesus works*. Once again, the Lord's half of the covenant is to provide what we ourselves lack—the power that turns honest effort into miracles.

THE SEALING COVENANT

We read at the beginning of this chapter that the highest degree of the celestial kingdom is reserved for those who enter into the new and everlasting covenant of marriage. Obviously, couples who are sealed together must be entering into some greater covenant, but what could be a greater commitment than the promises to live as Jesus lives and to work as Jesus works?

Actually, most Latter-day Saints seem content to equate a temple marriage with an extended-term civil marriage. Most of us contrast the *'til death do us part* clause in a civil marriage with the *for time and all eternity* clause in a temple marriage—and leave it at that. The hoped-for longevity of a temple marriage is certainly a precious blessing, but perhaps we are forgetting that covenants always involve promises made between two parties. When we present ourselves before God to be sealed, we are also promising something, and it is very important that we know what that promise is.

When I meet with temple-married couples in marital counseling, I sometimes will ask them if they can recall the vows they exchanged in the temple. Usually, they will suggest that they promised to live the law of chastity, to be faithful to each other.

21

Of course they have promised that, both at baptism and when they were endowed. However, the temple sealing ceremony does not address that topic at all.

This is a trick question, because we do not exchange vows while we are kneeling at that altar. In fact, we don't say anything to each other at all. Everything we say while we're at that altar is directed to the one who is officiating, and he is representing Heavenly Father. We are exchanging vows with God. If we keep our promises to Him, He promises us that we can someday have a forever family in the celestial kingdom and be able to live the life He lives. Our reward for keeping this great and last covenant is to receive "all things that the Father hath" (John 16:15).

So what is the new and everlasting covenant? When I was sealed to my wife, I promised Heavenly Father that I would receive her as He has received me.

Is this different from what couples promise each other when they exchange vows in a civil marriage? Of course it is. It is very different. If a couple contracts a marriage "not by me nor by my word" (D&C 132:15), they are making promises to each other before God, and not to God Himself. Not only does such a marriage lack the Lord's half of the covenant, but there is an altogether different understanding between husband and wife. In such a civil marriage, the bride and groom promise to bless each other's life only so long as they both honor their vows.

I will if you will. I'll be faithful to you if you are faithful to me. I'll earn a living if you greet me with a kiss when I come home. I'll do your laundry if you do the yard work. I'll comment on how nice you look if you make sure you never nag me. Few couples spell out in advance what they really envision as such a fair deal, but that doesn't really matter because no one is capable of living up to such an agreement after the infatuation period winds down anyway.

So what happens after the marriage has aged a little? The agreement begins to gradually turn upside down so that now it becomes: I won't be loyal to you because you weren't loyal to me. I won't bring home all of my paycheck because you didn't feel like being intimate with me last night. Your laundry can sit there and rot for all I care until you finally get off of that couch and go mow the lawn. No, I didn't notice that you changed your hairstyle because with your incessant nagging I'm trying to ignore you altogether.

How is this different from a temple marriage? If a couple really understands the covenants they make at the temple altar, there is no place for such an "if" clause in their relationship. Rather they will say, I'll turn away from flirtations because the Lord has received me, and I have taken His name. I'll deposit my full paycheck, and we'll balance the checkbook together because the Lord has received me, and the only way I can thank Him is by treating you as He treats me. I'll do your laundry because the Lord has received me, and the only way I can truly be His child is by blessing the one He has given me. I'll make the effort to notice how nice you look because the Lord has received me, and the only way I can return the love He has shown me is to show it to you.

What exactly do we covenant when we are sealed as spouses? We covenant to *love as Jesus loves!* We receive our spouse as Heavenly Father receives us. Despite all that has been written about self-esteem, "I love myself" is not going to fill the void that "you love me" fills. Anyone who says it can has simply despaired of sharing love with someone else. And we don't have to despair because, once again, the Lord will provide that which we ourselves lack—the power to become one with our spouses.

To love as Jesus loves is to bless someone else's life without expecting anything in return. It is to love those who have hurt you and who will hurt you again. It is even to forgive those who have hurt someone you love. Jesus taught us how to love:

> But love ye your enemies, and do good, and lend, hoping for nothing again; and your reward shall be great, and ye shall be the children of the Highest: for he is kind unto the unthankful and to the evil. Be ye therefore merciful, as your Father also is merciful. Judge not, and ye shall not be judged: condemn not,

and ye shall not be condemned: forgive, and ye shall
be forgiven: Give, and it shall be given unto you;
good measure, pressed down, and shaken together,
and running over, shall men give into your bosom.
For with the same measure that ye mete withal it
shall be measured to you again. (Luke 6:35–38)

LOVING AS JESUS LOVED

King Benjamin taught that "when ye are in the service
of your fellow beings ye are only in the service of your God"
(Mosiah 2:17). Jesus stated it even more powerfully: "Inasmuch
as ye have done it unto one of the least of these my brethren, ye
have done it unto me" (Matthew 25:40). When we help others, it
is counted as loving service to the Lord. Surely this applies even
more to how we treat our covenant partners!

There are many in the Church who have not been able to be
sealed to a worthy spouse. They may well feel that their personal
progression is at a standstill until they are able to receive this
ordinance. While it's true that they can hardly enjoy the blessings of marriage while they are single, this doesn't mean that
they can't grow by blessing the lives of others who are near to
them. The single aunt whose favorite nephew betrays her trust,
and whose faith in Christ leads her to forgive him, is loving as
Jesus loves. A single man who prays for the well-being of the
bride he hasn't met yet is also living this principle. Who can say
that the man who is married to a nonmember woman wouldn't
be blessed if he lives the principles of eternal marriage in anticipa-
tion of the covenant?

Is it harder or easier to love your spouse than it is to love
someone else? None of my neighbors, none of my coworkers,
none of my missionary companions, and none of my friends has
ever treated me as well as my wife has. On the other hand, none
of them is near enough to my heart to hurt me as much as she
can. Neither their words nor their actions can touch me as deeply
as her words and her actions do. Her loyalty is sweeter, but her
small betrayals are more bitter. I suppose that it's both harder and

easier to love those who are closest to us. Perhaps that's the reason marriage is particularly prone to ups and downs.

As a family therapist, I have seen families in distress, and it seems that some of the couples I've worked with are fulfilling Christ's description of family dysfunction: "And a man's foes shall be they of his own household" (Matthew 10:36). Nevertheless, His commandment has always been to love our enemies. I've found that those who can receive their spouses have hearts that work better than those who might be able to love others but who can't receive their spouses.

Jeff and Tammy

Jeff was the quintessential ward missionary. Not only was he spiritually prepared to teach gospel principles, but he was willing to be perpetually on call to the investigators he was teaching. He would often rush home from work and forego dinner with his family to make supplemental visits between the formal missionary lessons. Not surprisingly, Jeff realized considerable success in his calling, contributing to the conversions of whole families at a time! However, his enthusiasm for the work became coupled with frustration with his wife, Tammy, who began to complain that his calling had supplanted their marriage. He began to think of her as being dependent and non-supportive, and he found himself looking for reasons to be away from her.

To his credit, Jeff finally realized that he had dangerously drifted in his sealing covenant. He could see that he was losing his desire to receive his wife or for her to receive him. He made a prayerful effort to invest more of himself in his marriage, and within a short time, he rediscovered his love for Tammy. Jeff also found that the rest of his life worked better after he balanced his commitments. He felt temptations less keenly, and his evident loyalty to his marriage added to the attractiveness of the gospel message he was teaching.

Sometimes it is harder to love our spouses than it is to love others, yet learning to receive our companions will make our religion real as nothing else will. Nothing else will make us more

Christlike than to receive our spouses in the same new and everlasting covenant we have made with the Lord.

When I was baptized, I covenanted to live as Jesus lives, and I'm still growing in that principle. When I was endowed, I covenanted to work as Jesus works, and I'm still growing in that principle as well. Why should I be surprised that I must still grow in the principle of loving as Jesus loves and showing that love as I receive my wife?

But I *am* surprised. I'm surprised that receiving each other doesn't come easily or automatically. If someone really loves you, wouldn't they just naturally treat you lovingly every day of their lives? If that isn't how they always treat you, maybe they don't really love you after all! However, I don't believe many of us would apply such an unreasonable standard to those who were baptized (You mean, you still feel temptations?) or to those who have been endowed (You mean, you can't move mountains yet?).

However, that's exactly how most of us look at marriage. It must be either perfect from the outset or fatally flawed. When we discover that there will be rainy days along with the sunny ones, most of us begin to feel rather misused, cheated by fate, or stuck with an inferior product. We feel let down after discovering that the shiny bicycle in the ad arrives with some assembly required. After the first marital disagreement, many of us find our hopes deflated. We find out that marriage is work.

So we must either set ourselves to the task of growing into our covenants, or we must come up with a good excuse for doing something else. Too many of us opt for good excuses, and they come in three basic styles:

1. With a spouse like mine, I would only get hurt trying to make our marriage work.
2. There's too much water under the bridge, too much between us to ever make it work.
3. Perhaps it might have worked out, but one or both of us has already replaced our marriage with some other relationship or activity.

Those of us with such excuses are not looking for a way to save our marriages. Usually we're looking for permission to leave our marriages, or at least permission to turn oneness into coexistence.

Where is our faith? Three people can accomplish anything if one of them is Jesus Christ. We must look around us and see that many ideal couples were not always so happy. Surely they had their trials too. But they have overcome those trials by reaching out to the Savior for His healing grace—and that is what we all must do.

Robert and Annette

When their bishop first referred Robert and Annette for marriage counseling, it already seemed like a lost cause. They seemed so opposite in so many ways that the bishop wondered how they ever got together in the first place! Each was certain that their partner had somehow chosen to have an intolerable attitude, somehow decided to adopt an unreasonable point of view. Anytime either of them expressed unhappiness, the other felt compelled to point out that the problem would disappear if their partner would only see things their way. They had stopped making eye contact with each other for the last seven years of their ten-year marriage.

Their one child, Noel, knew he was loved by both of his parents, but he could sense the distance between them. Moreover, they seemed to be taking turns with him, rarely participating in any activity or conversation as a whole family. The bishop described Noel as a serious young man approaching baptism age, who somehow seemed to carry the weight of the world on his shoulders.

I felt sorry for all three of them. I shared the bishop's frustration that two reasonably likable people with no obvious handicaps should feel so hopeless about escaping from their world of quiet misery. Like most such couples, they couldn't see that the wall separating them from happiness was really not so very high nor so very thick. In fact, the wall might have fallen of its own accord had they not placed themselves on opposite sides, striving with all their might to push it down in opposite directions.

That they had remained stymied at this impasse for such a long time seemed proof to both of them that things would never change. What they didn't know was that the Lord was only waiting for them to come to Him for help, and then He would break down the wall. Coming unto Christ was the key. The question was never, "How can I change my spouse?" or even, "How can I change myself?" but rather, "What must I do to come unto Christ?"

The Lord allowed Robert and Annette to struggle for several more weeks before the Holy Spirit revealed the solution to that question. Perhaps the struggle is a necessary part of the process, because at the same time they received their answer, they also received the strength and desire to follow the prescribed course.

As you might suspect, the Lord didn't take sides. He didn't declare one of them to be more wrong than the other, nor did He help one of them see that the other's offenses weren't all that important. Instead, He touched Robert's heart to apologize for a bad choice of words, and He touched Annette's heart to thank Robert for doing so. Both little acts of charity would have cost them nothing if they had enjoyed a better relationship, but in this case, it took the Spirit of God to carry them past their wall, even for a few minutes.

These difficult acts of charity were not just a welcome reprieve from their punishing relationship; they were the key to a divine healing blessing. Such actions are the essence of coming unto Christ by becoming more like Christ, and that was the solution they had been praying for.

It seemed so simple later. The Lord wanted Robert to receive Annette, and the Lord wanted Annette to receive Robert, and both were worth receiving. The bishop had been telling them that for months, but until they came unto Christ, they just couldn't see it. Yet now, for just a moment seeing each other through the Lord's eyes, they were able to trust their partner. So lonely for so long, they could now begin to learn how to walk through life hand-in-hand.

Such moments began to come more often. They began to see that they were certainly different from one another, yet not necessarily opposite. Each an individual, yet both still within the range of normal or good enough. There was never any need to involve Noel in the therapy. Once his parents came together as a couple, he was free to be a child again, laying aside his role as the sole reason for the family's existence.

By fulfilling their side of the sealing covenant, Robert and Annette finally attained the promises they had received in the temple so many years before. It has been my privilege to witness this miracle in the lives of many couples. Once we know how to come unto Christ, we can receive the answers to our heart's deepest questions, and those answers come with the power to attain our heart's deepest desires.

As members of the Church, our part in the baptismal covenant is to strive to keep the commandments; Christ's part in the covenant is to empower us to keep the commandments through the gift of the Holy Spirit. As disciples, our part in the endowment covenant is to strive to magnify our callings; Christ's part in the covenant is to empower our weak efforts and bring forth the miracles. Finally, as heirs, our part in the sealing covenant is to strive to receive our spouses as the Lord receives us; Christ's part in the covenant is to empower us to overcome the fears, grudges, and divided loyalties that separate us from both His love and our love for one another.

Robert and Annette restored their temple marriage by coming unto Christ. They began to learn how to love as Jesus loves. In the next three chapters, we will examine how couples do this and how the Lord then blesses them to overcome the obstacles to oneness. The Lord alone has the power to do this. There simply is no other way.

*And the Lord appeared unto him the same night, and said,
I am the God of Abraham thy father: fear not, for I am
with thee, and will bless thee, and multiply thy seed for my
servant Abraham's sake.*

—Genesis 26:24

CHAPTER THREE
FEAR NOT,
FOR I AM WITH THEE

When Isaac and Rebekah and their twin sons, Esau and
Jacob, were forced by hard times to relocate to the land of the
Philistines, they said nothing about the Lord's promise that their
descendants would one day inherit the whole neighborhood.
Isaac was a little anxious about his new neighbors, enough so that
he lied to them about his pretty wife, fearing that one of them
might have killed him to marry his widow. Such worries did not
diminish after Isaac had grown rich among them and these same
neighbors suggested that he move out of town. This was Isaac's
situation at the time the Lord appeared to him and reassured him
that he need not fear, because he was not alone.

Isaac accepted this reassurance confidently, believing the Lord's promise that he and his family would be protected. As it turned out, his confidence was justified. Those neighbors soon offered a covenant of peace, and Isaac's worries seemed to be over. We like it when scripture stories turn out that way. We love to read where God's people rely on the Lord's promises and take the risks He asks them to and then come out okay in the end.

But most of us who have lived awhile have come to prefer reading such stories to actually living them out ourselves, because we've had a chance to witness the bad things that happen to good people. Sometimes cheaters win, the pure of heart have the strength of tin, and the bad guy gets the girl. We live in a scary world, and every one of us is going to get hurt once in a while— sometimes seriously, sometimes fatally.

On the other hand, we've seen instances where the Lord does protect His people. The Red Sea parted, Daniel's lions had their mouths closed, the angel opened Peter's prison cell, and the Mississippi River froze over! Miracles do happen, and they probably happen far more often than we realize. Many of us can recall occasions when the Lord has rescued us miraculously.

During my mission, I was asked one day to accompany another set of elders to visit a man who had been contacted that morning. He told them that he had studied Mormonism in some detail, and he wanted the answers to some specific questions. The elders knew I was a convert who could still recall what it was like to be an investigator, so they asked me to come along.

When we arrived that evening, we realized that some scripture authorities from his church had also been invited to meet with us. Moreover, he informed us that he had authored several anti-Mormon books and was in the process of writing another one. He placed a tape recorder on the table and turned it on, first asking me if I minded being quoted in his next book. The truth was I minded a lot! But I was only twenty at the time, and I foolishly thought missionaries were supposed to be able to handle any situation.

I reluctantly told him I didn't mind being tape-recorded, and

I quickly said a silent prayer that nothing I said would ever hurt the Church. He seemed pleased with my attitude, and he proceeded to ask his first question. I don't recall what it was, but it was heavily laden with innuendo, and I began to answer the best I could. I could soon tell, however, that my answer was coming out wrong, and that I was frankly outclassed in this contest. Things were not looking good.

At that moment, I began to smell burning wires, and we all realized that the tape recorder had stopped running. The man tried to get it started again a few more times, and then he gave up on recording my answers. I offered a silent prayer of thanks, and I was still more grateful a few minutes later when he decided to postpone the interview for another day. Naturally, that was the last meeting any of us had with that fellow. It may have been just a small miracle, but it was a miracle nonetheless, and we all knew it.

We know that the Lord can protect us, but will He? Unless we're inspired beforehand that the Lord will intervene, we don't really know if the upcoming story will be one of justified faith or of sanctified sacrifice. Will we be saved by God's power in the nick of time, or will we be martyrs who were faithful to the end? Daniel's three friends were spared the fiery furnace, but the believers in Ammonihah were not. Faith and sacrifice are both true principles, and both show up in all of our lives.

Keeping our covenants is often a question of facing our fears. It is significant that the Lord's reassurance to Isaac was simply, "I am with thee." We spoke in the last chapter of holding the Savior's hand as we struggle with a temptation, call down a miracle in the ministry, or bless an enemy. We can do anything if we feel His presence with us; we don't have to face our enemies alone. The Spirit can reveal to our spirits that Jesus is at our side, just on the other side of the veil. He may or may not protect us from harm, but either way He will stand by us until it is over.

I have seen many instances where men, women, and children have been brave in the face of imminent pain, and it was obvious that their courage came from their relationship with the Savior.

I know a man who received his wife back into his home after her affair failed, even though she seemed certain to leave again as soon as she could arrange it. I recall when a woman learned of her husband's lifelong destructive addiction but decided to stand by him and stick it out. I know of a child who voluntarily returned to live with her brutal parents over the protest of counselors who warned her that things would probably get even worse. In each case, I wasn't sure these people were doing the wise thing, but I knew they were doing the brave thing as they each followed what they believed to be personal revelation.

On the other hand, it matters that we do the right thing, that we distinguish personal revelation from blind faith. The Apostle Peter gave us a good example of this principle. When he saw the Savior walking upon the water, he said, "Lord, if it be thou, bid me come unto thee on the water" (Matthew 14:28). Peter didn't just close his eyes, leap out of the boat, and hope to find sure footing amidst the waves. He first made sure the Lord wanted him to walk on the water. Not until Jesus said "Come" did Peter take the first step.

We likewise should not assume that God will make everything work out until we are certain He has told us so. Our faith is that God can guide our steps and that most of the time He will lead us away from danger. We should not take unnecessary chances and expect God to rescue us over and over again. We're not required to take stupid risks for the sake of being valiant.

However, we are required to take significant risks for the sake of keeping our covenants. For those with temple marriages, one of those covenants is to receive our spouses as Jesus receives us. We covenant to treat our eternal partners as we would treat the Lord Himself, yet we can't always tell if our spouse is striving to do the same. What if my spouse's plan is to treat me no better—and perhaps even worse—than I deserve to be treated? What if my spouse has lost the desire to show love to the Lord by showing love to me? How lopsided a relationship am I willing to tolerate? In facing my fear, I must ask myself, "What is it I'm afraid of? What's the worst thing that can happen?"

Many painful things can happen. I could lose my security. I might be forced to give up my sweetest dream and my fondest desire. I might feel stupid. I might be physically injured. I might be betrayed by the one I love most. I might be publicly humiliated. I might be abandoned. Someone else that I love might be injured. These fears are both realistic and significant, and each of them would really hurt.

Are we willing to hold the Savior's hand as we face these fears, or will we opt for the excuse that "with a spouse like mine, I would only get hurt trying to make our marriage work?" We're certainly under no obligation to let our spouses destroy us, but too many of us abandon a temple marriage after no worse than disappointment and hurt feelings! The Lord never promised us that married life would be free of disappointment and hurt feelings.

FACING THE SMALLER FEARS IN OUR MARRIAGES

Sometimes, no more than the threat of bad news is sufficient to cause us to withdraw from the one who might hurt us. We become distant, avoid eye contact, and practice selective listening—lest we see what we don't want to see and hear what we don't want to hear. There are times, however, when the emergency state we create is unnecessary, because the feared attack isn't being planned after all.

Brent and Janice

Brent and Janice had only been married a few months. Both had enjoyed very active social lives prior to meeting each other. But while Janice had always cut her ties with previous boyfriends, Brent regularly converted romances into lasting friendships. After they were married, Janice told Brent that she expected him to end these friendships, and she became distressed when he told her he didn't want to do that. They began discussing divorce but decided they would seek marital counseling first.

In the first session, it became clear that they each understood her ultimatum differently. Brent thought Janice was forbidding him to ever have any other friends at all, whereas she was only asking him to add a discreet distance in his friendships with former girlfriends. They agreed to concentrate on couple friends as they adjusted to their new marriage, and both felt comfortable enough with this compromise that no further counseling seemed necessary. In this instance, the emergency state that Brent and Janice had created was premature. Neither of them wanted to hurt the other, yet both were afraid of being stuck in a bad marriage. Sometimes fear is the problem.

Guardrail: Levels of Conflict

Sometimes a couple's confidence in their marriage collapses as they begin to experience conflict with each other. No relationship is without some conflict, and couples who learn to identify the level of conflict are usually better able to defuse escalating tension. At its least serious level, there is simply a *discussion,* where a couple might agree on some issues but not on others. The next level is a *disagreement,* where the situation calls for either agreement or compromise but where there's no serious threat to each person's feelings for one another. The third level is an *argument,* where it's not okay to disagree on the topic and where both individuals try to defend their position so their partner will agree or give in. The situation deteriorates quickly as couples move to the fourth level, a *quarrel,* where the focus turns from the topic of disagreement to their opinion of each other and where they don't particularly want to be quoted as they defend themselves to the death. Even more serious is the fifth level, a *shutdown,* where they altogether give up on a resolution and simply do whatever it takes to get their partner to either acquiesce or leave for awhile. Paradoxically, the most serious level of conflict, *disengagement,* is also the quietest, since at least one partner no longer cares what the other thinks or feels.

It's unusual for one person to operate more than one level away from their partner. More typically, both spouses are equally engaged in the dance at near the same level of conflict, and it doesn't help too much to worry about which one moved to a more serious level first. It's more helpful that they analyze what happened later, after they've both cooled down, and then name the level of conflict.

That shifts the question away from "What sort of person am I married to?" and moves toward "What are we doing to each other?" If I can help my clients distinguish how they progress from one level of conflict to another, they often see that their partner is not out to get them or is totally unreasonable, but only that they've developed a bad habit as a couple. This perspective can neutralize a lot of fear in a marriage.

Guardrail: Time-Out Walk

I've discovered an exercise that can serve as a guardrail for couples who too easily shift to more serious levels of conflict. I ask the one who first senses the escalation of tension to call a time out, offering to take a five-minute walk around the block (ensuring personal safety, of course), and promising to resume the discussion immediately afterward. If after the partner's return, tensions again begin to mount, it will be the other's turn to take the walk. And so on. I've yet to meet the couple willing to take more than two turns each. Almost always they learn to take a deep breath, calm down, and resume their discussion without taking more walks.

Guardrail: Six-Shooters

Many would protest, however, that it's nearly impossible to reduce the level of conflict when your partner is saying such hurtful things. In marriage particularly, it often seems that there's a painful word fight that never quite ends. It's as though each spouse carries a six-shooter in each holster and alternately shoots the other with one pistol called *shame* and the other pistol called *guilt.*

We're struck with a shame bullet every time we're told, "You should have made things right, but you couldn't do that— because you're a little weakling." We're struck with a guilt bullet every time we're told, "You had the power to make things right, but you chose not to do that—because you're a big bad meanie!" Don't we almost hear the blaming parental voice and the whining child voice?

We usually return fire with the same pistol we were shot with. Using the shame gun, "We wouldn't have run out of gas if you hadn't forgotten again to fill the car yesterday! (You ineffectual dolt!)." Using the guilt gun, "I only raised my voice because you weren't listening! (I guess my opinion doesn't matter, Mr. Know-it-all)."

Then if that doesn't work, we usually switch guns. Using the guilt gun, "Oh, I know. It's my fault we ran out of gas. Everything is always my fault! (I think I'm going to cry)." Using the shame gun, "You never listen. That's why no one likes talking with you! (Now you don't feel so big, do you?)."

Another guardrail couples can use to end this word fight is simply to practice recognizing which bullet they've just been shot with and which bullet they've just shot back. After awhile, both spouses can catch themselves right after firing, take it back, and figuratively return both pistols to their holsters and hold their hands out to the side in a gesture of peace: "Wait. I'm sorry. I didn't mean that." Many times, couples who learn to communicate as adult equals develop more confidence in their ability to resolve conflicts together.

Sometimes spouses are paralyzed by inverse fears. She's terrified of abandonment, but he panics at the thought of being smothered by dependency. He becomes anxious in the face of ambiguity, yet she feels incapable of self-disclosure. She fears that if they lose control over their children's behavior, they will lose the children as well, while he fears that overcontrol will drive their children away. His confidence in finding a new job collapses when she turns away from him, yet pulling the blanket over her head is the only way she knows to deal with losing her economic security. In each case, neither party wants to hurt the other, yet they both see the other as the source of their own pain.

These are still the easier cases, where there is no intent to harm. When both spouses realize that neither wants the other to hurt and that they both still want to receive each other, they can usually agree on a compromise that offers some reassurance to both of them. The key to counseling such couples is to help them see that neither of them would be satisfied with a solution that leaves their partner fearful or in pain.

A wife can accept the fact that her husband likes time alone after coming home from work, because she knows he'll ask her to take a walk with him after dinner. He won't expect an immediate answer to one of his probing questions, because he knows she'll answer him in a letter before the week is up. She'll accept his mediation in a conflict with the children, knowing that he'll always support her if they come to him to complain about her. He'll acknowledge that she's not ever going to initiate physical intimacy during the period of his unemployment, but he'll also appreciate that she does accept him each time he reaches out to her.

Marriage is often a case of compromise, a balance of each other's wishes. Couples may choose to renegotiate the midpoint of these compromises from time to time, however, since it's human nature to overestimate our own pain and to underestimate someone else's pain. We tend to repeat the question, "Is it really that important for you?"

But in these cases, it's likely that the same love that led them to give in a little in the first place will lead them to do so again. These are the cases that are the most fun for a marriage counselor, because the resolution is accomplished quickly, and because the relief is so palpable when they come to realize that they do love each other after all.

It's significantly more difficult when couples with inverse fears become polarized in their relationship. They come to think of themselves as opposites instead of merely different. They perceive their own position as well within the normal range, yet see their partner's position as extreme and unreasonable. Often they fear that their companion is both insatiable and unwilling to compromise.

For example, suppose I'm more concerned about reducing debt than about increasing savings, while my wife is more anxious about having enough savings than about having too much debt. We both fall within the normal range, however, so that both of us would choose to carry some consumer debt and yet still have some savings.

But what if one or the other of us begins to fear that we're married to an extremist? What if she begins to think that I don't care at all about savings, while I conclude that she doesn't care at all about our debt load? What if I come to believe that nothing but my constant vigilance keeps us solvent, while she clearly sees that her nagging alone provides us with a future? Most couples who become polarized this way will usually begin to test each other. It's been my experience that the spouse almost always fails the test! The reason for this is found in the nature of most testing.

If I want to test the hypothesis that my wife doesn't care at all about our debt load, then I might innocently suggest that we should just put our entire income tax refund into savings this year. I'm hoping she'll realize how irresponsible this is and counter my suggestion with a proposal to put part into savings and part toward the debt. But I won't tell her that. By being unexpectedly agreeable about the matter, I try my best to carry off the impression that it's okay with me either way.

The problem with this deception is that she's bound to misunderstand me, and she'll conclude that—for some strange reason—I've finally begun to value how important it is to have a good savings program. When she happily makes the choice I've asked her to make, I leap to the unfounded conclusion that she wants only savings and no debt relief. And now, having proven my case, I'm not likely to listen when she tells me that she isn't as extreme as I'm seeing her, that she also values what's important to me—just not as much.

On the other hand, the depth of my hurt feelings will surely seem hard evidence to her that I'm the extremist. She'll assume that if I had my way, we wouldn't put one dollar of that income tax refund into savings! She may even conclude that she herself must be an extremist after all, since she's obviously opposite from me. "Yes," she might declare, "I don't care anything about paying off debts when our savings is so small!"

Guardrail: Sign-Off Book

I've discovered another exercise that can serve as a guardrail for couples who have become polarized regarding a particular issue, such as parenting, sex, or—as in the above example—finances. I ask them to play a game for two weeks: they must come to an agreement regarding each and every decision pertaining to the issue at hand before taking any action at all. They will note in a spiral notebook what they have agreed upon, and both will sign off on each decision, whereupon neither can complain about that particular decision ever again.

They always have the option of not agreeing, of course, but they must take no action at all if that is the case. If discussion isn't possible and yet action must be taken, then the one making the decision should note in the spiral notebook their best estimate of what their partner would judge to be the best choice—and then take that action, with the other spouse reviewing and signing off on the decision after his or her return.

In the above example, the couple would need to discuss and agree before making any purchase, deposit, withdrawal, or investment. They could not so much as purchase a candy bar without agreeing together to do so, and noting that decision in their spiral notebook. If circumstances prevent their discussing a purchase that absolutely must be made now, then the one making the purchase will have to act in good faith, following their best estimate of what their partner would choose to do if it were his or her decision alone.

The effectiveness of this exercise becomes most apparent with those unilateral decisions, because the returning spouse learns just how extreme their partner judges them to be. "You really thought I would have made that decision? I'm not that crazy. I wonder if I'd do any better guessing what your true opinion is.

Maybe neither one of us is so extreme after all." This exercise has helped many couples see each other in a new light, as different from each other perhaps, yet still both within the normal range.

It's very important that married couples learn to recognize when they've become polarized. Very few couples are truly opposites, but many couples come to believe they are. And once that fear is well-established, it can infect the whole relationship.

Spouses need to realize that there's no better way of knowing what their partner feels—or what their partner intended—than to simply ask. And then to ask clarifying questions for a fuller understanding. And then to believe what is said. It's a daunting task, but the Lord will stand at our side as we confront this fear. He always has.

FACING REAL DANGER IN OUR MARRIAGES

Much more serious are those marriages where one or both partners intentionally harms the other, or where they want everything their own way whether it hurts their partner or not. Such a disregard for each other's pain is the surest sign that a marriage is in real trouble. In these marriages, at least one of the partners really doesn't care, and perhaps never did. Sooner or later, some of their partner's worst fears might be realized in such a marriage: frustration, humiliation, abandonment, betrayal, and even bodily injury.

During my mission, we met a woman who seemed sincerely interested in reading the Book of Mormon and who invited us back to present the missionary lessons. When we returned, however, she seemed to be ignoring our knock. When she finally answered the door, we discovered why she had not wanted us to see her. She had been savagely beaten by her husband and had deep cuts about her face and head and a severely bruised and swollen cheek. She told us that he had a terrible temper. She wasn't even sure why he had beaten her this time (we were relieved to learn it had nothing to do with our visit), but she was certain she'd done nothing to merit his anger.

Perhaps most bitter to her was the knowledge that he felt

absolutely no remorse for treating her so. As far as she knew, he simply chose from time to time to vent his feelings in that fashion. We offered to find her a ride to a women's shelter, but she wouldn't hear of it. She said she loved him, even though he obviously didn't love her.

What obligation does she have to receive a spouse who would hurt her so, with neither forbearance beforehand nor regret afterward? If she ever escaped from such a situation, would the Lord expect her to submit to it again? Would her obligation have been any different if she had been sealed to her husband, instead of only civilly married? What does someone do who is stuck in a bad marriage, trembling under the threat of her worst fears, wishing that more time had been taken in deciding when to get married and to whom?

The answer to these questions is found in the Sermon on the Mount, that sure foundation of all Christian belief. Jesus said, "Ye have heard that it hath been said, Thou shalt love thy neighbour, and hate thine enemy. But I say unto you, Love your enemies, bless them that curse you, do good to them that hate you, and pray for them which despitefully use you, and persecute you; that ye may be the children of your Father which is in heaven" (Matthew 5:43–45).

An abused spouse may think, "I want to be a child of God, and if the only way to become a child of God is to love my enemy, I may just have to learn how to do it. The Lord said that I must bless them that curse me; so I should say something nice to (or about) someone who has hurt me with his words. He also said that I must do good to them that hate me; so I should do something nice to someone who did me dirt. Then He said that I should pray for someone who used me despitefully or persecuted me; so even if someone is on a search and destroy mission and I'm running for my life, I'm supposed to be praying for him as I run."

But wait a minute. I don't want to do any of those things! I don't want to go anywhere near that guy; after all, he just hurt me! I don't want to pray for him; I don't even want to think about him. Why would my Savior ask me to show compassion for someone who has hurt me? I can't see how it's going to make me feel any better, and I really don't think it's going to bring about that fellow's reformation either! It isn't fair at all.

The key is that the Lord is going to be there to help me confront even my worst fears. He has said, "Wherefore, be of good cheer, and do not fear, for I the Lord am with you, and will stand by you" (D&C 68:6). He doesn't want me to live out my life in fear. The truth is that if I'll hold His hand while returning good for evil, I can be healed of what might otherwise be a lifelong paralyzing fear.

But how do I hold the Savior's hand? Is this just a comforting metaphor? I have learned that when I face unavoidable danger, I must ask the Lord for His presence, because I know I can't handle it alone. When I have done this, I've sensed the presence of God and felt calmed by the Holy Spirit, and then I've felt strong enough to do what I have to do. This is one of the everyday miracles of Christianity, something I can count on every time I extend myself to do what Jesus has asked me to do. He may or may not rescue me from the danger, but He will always rescue me from my fear of facing it alone.

It seems our investigator had the right to flee to the women's shelter after all, but then her Christian duty would have been to sincerely pray for the husband who had so despitefully used her. Of course, this would be a very difficult assignment, not less so as she sorted through her feelings and discovered her natural rage at how she'd been treated. She would have had to ask the Lord for an extra dose of charity before she could pray for him with any sincerity.

But in return, she would have received the comforting awareness that she need not fear her husband's wrath or her own indigent situation. Her husband might never know how she had blessed him, and he would not likely have cared had he known. In praying for him, she would be the one to receive the blessing.

In this case, there would have been no difference in her duty, even if she had been sealed to him in the temple. She would have been obligated to receive him as far as she was able, but his dangerous behavior would have limited that reception to the safety of her own prayers anyway. The only difference in the situation would be that the Lord would surely come down harder on her husband if he were a priesthood holder who was guilty of such wickedness. Concerning such men or women who grievously offend their covenants, the Lord has said, "[If] he or she shall commit any sin or transgression of the new and everlasting covenant whatever . . . they shall be destroyed in the flesh, and shall be delivered unto the buffetings of Satan unto the day of redemption" (D&C 132:26).

No one who treats others unkindly deserves to receive good in return; this has nothing at all to do with fairness. This is simply another, more serious, application of our covenant to love as Jesus loves. This is not, however, an expectation that either the husband or the wife should be a doormat for the other, or that either is obligated to always let the other one have his way.

Rather, we are discussing a freewill offering, a single action or a series of actions to cleanse our own hearts of fear, resentment, and selfishness, allowing us to love as Jesus loves. This offering cannot be expected or demanded. If so, it would constitute the first mile, not the second. Furthermore, it is absolutely unimportant whether the recipient ever knows that the freewill offering is made. This is not about changing someone else's heart. It's about changing our own heart. It's about healing.

Randy and Sarah

Randy and Sarah had a temple marriage, but they were anything but happy. Sarah was a convert who had been very careful to date only returned missionaries, and she felt sure that Randy was the caliber of man she wanted as a husband. He was hardworking, thoughtful, and nonjudgmental, and these qualities were very important to her. However, Sarah had a short temper, and she assumed that Randy would gently confront and control her moodiness as her father had always been able to do.

That wasn't Randy's strong suit. When Sarah became irritable and complaining, he would generally find some excuse to leave the house and wait for the storm to blow over. After a short time, Sarah began to lose respect for Randy, and she concluded that he was no man at all. She began to find fault with nearly everything Randy did, and he came to dread being around her. Their relationship was on a downward spiral.

Sarah refused to accompany Randy to counseling, but he and I met together, and we concluded that his tendency to retreat left Sarah feeling abandoned. Randy recognized that he was afraid of women's emotions, particularly their angry emotions. We rehearsed how he might respond differently when she became angry. Randy could remain in the room, listen to Sarah's complaints, and show her that he understood what she was saying, even if he might not agree entirely with everything she said.

Randy could picture responding this way, and he committed to try. He failed. After a week, it became obvious that he simply lacked the courage to face something he had always run away from. Randy concluded that his only option was to enjoy Sarah when she was happy, avoid her when she was angry, and accept the fact that she didn't respect him. Then we talked together about his testimony of the Savior and how he had confronted other fears when he was on his mission. Randy began a fast, and he prayed to feel the Holy Spirit's presence the next time Sarah lost her temper.

He didn't have long to wait. That evening, Sarah loudly complained that no one else ever did the dishes and the kitchen was a mess! Whereas he ordinarily would have tuned her out as he watched television, this time Randy turned off the set and gave Sarah his full attention. Having an audience, Sarah warmed to the subject and reviewed a wide range of complaints, returning again and again to Randy's inadequacies. He listened patiently. He maintained eye contact most of the time. Randy was surprised that, for once, he felt little desire to flee. This time he felt the Savior comforting and sustaining him.

Randy suddenly saw the request for help hidden within Sarah's anger. She needed his presence in her day-to-day life the same way Randy needed the Savior's presence. Randy reached out to comfort Sarah, and in the very act of doing so felt his own fear diminish further. He asked her if she would like to do the dishes together, and Sarah agreed.

After a few minutes, Sarah apologized to Randy for her harsh words. That was important to Randy, but more important was the fact that he had faced his fear squarely. He had done the impossible. He had found the Savior's strength as he held the Savior's hand.

WE CAN STILL KEEP THE COVENANT

Every so often, a grieved spouse asks whether a temple marriage should end in a civil divorce. I've never felt it was my place to answer that question, but I have sometimes advised a client to seek physical safety while she is answering that question herself. I do believe that Heavenly Father is the only one who can authorize a civil divorce and that anyone contemplating this action should be very sure of divine revelation beforehand. We all feel a sense of relief when we lay down a frustrating problem, but that is no sure sign of heavenly direction. We must not confuse relief with inspiration.

Unquestionably, there are times when the Lord will direct a civil divorce. These are the blessedly rare cases where one or both spouses pose a significant physical or spiritual threat to each other or their children. On the other hand, contention in the home doesn't necessarily justify a civil divorce. Many persons claim that they divorced for the sake of the children, but often this is only replacing one form of unhappiness with another. Few children from divorced homes consider their's a happy childhood. Couples should be very cautious before ending a temple marriage.

It is significant that there is no automatic sealing cancellation following a civil divorce. In fact, such a cancellation is difficult to obtain, usually only granted when the woman is prepared to be sealed to another worthy man after her first sealing is canceled. Until she does so, canceling this ordinance would serve no useful purpose for either one of them. While they are still sealed together, they can merit eternal blessings by loving as Jesus loves.

Even after a civil divorce, what would prevent them from offering to make home repairs, being regular in child-support payments, or encouraging their children to love both parents by making visitation with them as pleasant as possible? We can still keep the covenant. We don't have to live together, or even be in love to treat each other as Christ would.

John and Barbara

Barbara was involved in an extramarital affair with John, which contributed heavily to the breakup of her temple marriage. She justified herself in the thought that her ex-husband was also partly responsible for the divorce, and she and John eventually formed a very successful civil marriage. Barbara was excommunicated from the Church, but she shared her faith with John, and he joined the Church some years before she was rebaptized.

They have now been faithful members of the Church for many years, yet they understand that Church policy generally prohibits the sealing of adulterers who break up a temple marriage. Exceptions are rare and must come from the First Presidency. They are hoping that there will be some provision in the next world for them to realize this blessing.

John and Barbara now wish they had repented before her divorce. Had they done so, they would have broken off their affair and preserved Barbara's temple marriage. It's painful for them to consider what life would have been like without each other, but even harder is the realization that they destroyed something eternal. Through the years of waiting for this blessing together, they have grown to appreciate the holiness of this ordinance, and they told me that now they would not hurt a temple marriage for anything.

Why did Barbara end her temple marriage in the first place? She and her first husband had grown apart, and Barbara felt helpless to recapture their loving feelings. Her faith in the Savior was no match against her fear of loneliness, and replacing her husband required less courage than repairing her temple marriage.

Barbara now knows that the Savior could have healed the rift in her first marriage. The Lord has strengthened her to face other difficult situations, and He would have strengthened her then. Barbara and John now live by their convictions courageously; they wish they had been braver then.

Others who buckle under their fears are the single men and women who indefinitely postpone a temple marriage rather than risk one that might not work out. Many point to the failed marriages of parents or other heroes, or they keep score between the temple marriages that lead to oneness versus those that don't. If they do date someone with serious marriage potential, they may adopt such unrealistically high standards for their relationship that neither they nor their partners can ever measure up. Less obvious are those who are civilly married to nonmembers, who covertly discourage the conversion of their spouses. There are many ways that our fears can stand between us and exaltation.

WE WILL NOT BE ALONE

As we confront such fears, our Savior invites us to lean upon His arm, to let Him steady our hearts. His atonement provided a way for Him to share our painful burdens, and like Alma's people in the Book of Mormon, we can receive divine strength to endure what we fear so much:

> And it came to pass that the voice of the Lord came to them in their afflictions, saying: Lift up your heads and be of good comfort, for I know of the covenant which ye have made unto me; and I will covenant with my people and deliver them out of their bondage. And I will also ease the burdens which are put upon your shoulders, that even you cannot feel them upon your backs, even while you are in bondage; and this will I do that ye may stand as witnesses for me hereafter, and that ye may know of a surety that I, the Lord God, do visit my people in their afflictions. (Mosiah 24:13–14)

Furthermore, He has promised that our injuries are only temporary. Like our sins, our emotional wounds can heal until they lose their immediacy, until "[we] remember [our] pains no more" (Alma 36:19). What's more, we have a promise that the last trace of our emotional scars will heal over and disappear in the Resurrection:

> And God shall wipe away all tears from their eyes; and there shall be no more death, neither sorrow, nor crying, neither shall there be any more pain: for the former things are passed away. And he that sat upon the throne said, Behold, I make all things new. (Revelation 21:4–5)

The Apostle John said, "There is no fear in love; but perfect love casteth out fear" (1 John 4:18). If we let the Lord guide us, we can recognize who, when, and where we should marry. Moreover, we can keep those temple marriages alive by blessing our partners as the Lord blesses us. When our spouses disappoint us or treat us unkindly, we can still merit the blessings of eternal life by returning good for evil. This principle applies even when perilous circumstances require a marital separation.

We live in a dangerous world, but we are not alone. The Savior has made great promises to "the children of the covenant" (3 Nephi 20:26). He offers us comfort and direction now and an eternal reward with Him in the next world. We can obtain healing in this life and complete renewal in the life to come. The Lord's voice is unto all of us, saying, "Fear not, for I am with thee."

If he hath wronged thee, or oweth thee ought, put that on
mine account; I Paul have written it with mine own hand, I
will repay it; albeit I do not say to thee how thou owest unto
me even thine own self besides.

—Philemon 18–19

CHAPTER FOUR
PUT THAT
ON MY ACCOUNT

The Apostle Paul was a prisoner in Rome when he introduced a runaway slave, Onesimus, to the gospel of Jesus Christ. Ordinarily, this would have been an entirely joyous event, but there was a twist to this conversion story: Another of Paul's converts, Philemon, was the former slave master, and he wanted Onesimus back!

Paul taught that God is no respecter of persons, and it's evident that the low status of slaves meant nothing to him personally. Nevertheless, Paul believed in obeying the law, and it was against the law for slaves to abscond from their masters. That was the dilemma: Should Paul turn his new friend in to the authorities? Should Onesimus voluntarily return to slavery? Should Philemon let his other slaves see that conversion to Christianity is the quick road out of slavery?

Paul finally concluded on the ingenious plan of sending Onesimus back home with a letter asking Philemon to accept him as Paul's son and to free Onesimus as a favor to Paul. This would leave Paul an honest man, Onesimus a free man, Philemon a generous man, and Greek society intact. There was no reason why this solution shouldn't have resolved the situation to everyone's satisfaction, provided Philemon was in a forgiving mood.

It's significant that Paul didn't entirely leave it up to Philemon's best judgment but included in his letter the argument that Philemon owed it to him. Paul pointed out that this was the very least that Philemon could do for the missionary who had brought the gospel message to him. There was a cash balance on Paul's debit card, and this favor he was asking was already prepaid. He didn't have to remind Philemon that he owed much to Paul, "even thine own self besides" (Philemon 18), and now all he was asking was for Philemon to "put that on mine account."

Given that the loss of a slave was a serious financial setback, and granted that Philemon had done nothing to merit such an unfair loss (we'll have to suspend judgment for now on the relative fairness of slavery in general), shouldn't Philemon's sense of gratitude cancel out his sense of injustice? That seemed to be the gist of Paul's argument.

TREATING A GRUDGE

Is that the way we handle grudges? When we suffer unfair treatment from someone, are we supposed to just count our many blessings and remind ourselves of those who have done us favors? Will this cancel out our feelings of resentment? It sounds pretty good in theory, but do people really work that way? My parents sure did a lot for me; I owe them so much I should be able to forgive just about anything that will ever happen to me.

That isn't how it's worked out in my life. On those occasions when I've felt angry and misused, I never saw any connection between the person I was angry with and other people who had previously been nice to me. I wanted justice or revenge, or at least understanding and sympathy.

Furthermore, when someone pointed out to me that I might have misunderstood or misjudged my enemy's intentions, or reminded me that I'd done the same thing myself, my first response was hardly a sigh of relief that I could now lay down my resentment. No, my first response was to look upon my new counselor as a collaborator with the enemy.

On the other hand, there have been times when I suddenly realized that I was misreading things and that I was the one who was to blame. I reprimand the children for leaving the door open, and I scold them for letting the cooler air escape, only to recall that I had left it open myself a few minutes ago while carrying in the groceries. I mutter angrily at the driver who cut me off when I was trying to change lanes, only to remember that my left turn signal indicator isn't working. I carry on about the evident inefficiency of the state office that has taken so long to process an application, and then I find the unmailed envelope in my box.

I feel terrible at times like that. I'm suddenly filled with a desire for tolerance and understanding toward all, and this feeling can spill over to cancel out a few unrelated grudges as well. At that instant, I would be prepared to forgive two or three slaves for running away! And if those around me catch the spirit of tolerance and forgive me for my faults, I begin to feel some of the gratitude Paul was talking about.

But I only have such feelings when I can see that I'm in the wrong. More frequent are the times when I feel like Philemon. I can't see that I've done anything wrong, and I'm quite certain that someone has done something wrong to me. It really matters at such times how close to my heart was the blow, how intentional the offense was, and whether insult was added to the injury.

How long does a grudge last? I believe most of us have drawn a line in the sand, and we're prepared to forgive and forget offenses that are less serious than a certain point. But offenses that are more serious than that point seem to have a half-life of centuries! Most of us can easily recall a few instances where someone really did us dirt, and the wound still feels fresh even after many years.

If I'm not careful, an assessment interview can quickly turn into a rehearsal of every grudge the client has been nursing throughout their life. There was the guy who cheated his co-worker out of a promotion with back-stabbing gossip. There was the best friend who felt it her duty to let everyone in the ward know her friend's son had been apprehended smoking marijuana. There was the driver of the other car who had been drinking before the crash that killed a local high school student. There was the former wife who refused a father visitation with his children during his first and only period of unemployment since the divorce.

These stories seem just as poignant fifteen years later as they were at the time the offense occurred. What do we have to do to let these things go? We might try to avert our attention from the grievance, remove ourselves from the one who offended us, or try to think about something else. But what do you do if the one who offended you is living with you? What if it's the person you're sealed to for time and all eternity?

Jesus has provided us a way to lay down the awful weight of our grudges. He said, "Take my yoke upon you, and learn of me; for I am meek and lowly in heart: and ye shall find rest unto your souls. For my yoke is easy, and my burden is light" (Matthew 11:29–30).

Anyone who has carried a heavy grudge can appreciate this marvelous promise. It's been said that a clear conscience can make our sleep sweet; the same thing can be said for relinquishing our grievances. So many of us nurse our grudges and keep them white hot in our hearts. Wouldn't it be a relief for these memories to fade into old news? The Lord can heal our hearts, and a painful memory can come to feel like a dream, or like something that happened long ago to someone else. That's what healing feels like.

Jesus also taught that those who remove their heart-bound

burdens may also be blessed with clearer vision:

"And why beholdest thou the mote that is in thy brother's eye, but considerest not the beam that is in thine own eye? Or how wilt thou say to thy brother, Let me pull out the mote out of thine eye; and, behold, a beam is in thine own eye? Thou hypocrite, first cast out the beam out of thine own eye; and then shalt thou see clearly to cast out the mote out of thy brother's eye" (Matthew 7:3–5).

Many of my clients have felt that they can communicate with absolutely anyone in the world—except the spouse they are sealed to. It seems to them that, no matter how hard they try, they are speaking two different languages. Their husband or wife is inevitably going to misread whatever they are trying to say. Of course, there are some people who deliberately twist what their partners say just to torment them, but there are many more who try as hard as they can to communicate—and it just doesn't work.

Oh, to be able to see clearly! Most of us would be happy to see what was going on at all, whether we could communicate or not. But if we could finally understand one another, that would really be wonderful! And it appears that this is exactly what the Savior is promising. So, what is it we must do to lay down our yoke and remove the beam from our eye?

THE SECOND-MILE OFFERING

We must do the same thing to heal our grudges that we do to heal our fears. We must bless our enemies. In the last chapter, we discussed how Jesus taught, "Ye have heard that it hath been said, Thou shalt love thy neighbour, and hate thine enemy. But I say unto you, Love your enemies, bless them that curse you, do good to them that hate you, and pray for them which despitefully use you, and persecute you; that ye may be the children of your Father which is in heaven" (Matthew 5:43–45).

We will never get peace in this life by running away from the twin monsters of fear and resentment. We only get peace as we take the Savior's hand, go back to the field of battle, and return a blessing for the hurt that was done to us. It is a very challenging assignment. For most of us, the only way to truly bless our enemies is to do for them the last thing that we would ever choose to do.

Many of my clients have stood at this precipice of decision, wrestling with themselves as to whether the antidote to resentment is more painful than the poison, who finally concluded that they have always known what they must do. I can't tell them what they should do. They have to tell me. And they generally do.

The Lord might want them to do something as simple as a genuine compliment or an unexpected favor. It may be to extend another invitation with the expectation of being rebuffed again. It might be to write a letter explaining events from your adversary's point of view. Very often, it is no harder than making a request so clearly that the other person knows what you're asking for. None of these things may seem very difficult. They are only hard to do because our hearts are bound by feelings of resentment.

But sometimes the task is something that would be difficult for anyone to do. It may be to correct an error in a project and save your hypercritical supervisor from losing his job. It could be to sustain a bishop whose insensitivity contributed to your daughter leaving the Church. It might be to let your teenage son go live with your ex-husband and his new wife. The Lord forgave the very soldiers who crucified Him; we can't be sure that He won't ask something hard of us.

To overcome my resentment, I must truly bless the one who misused me. It isn't necessarily something my adversary would ask for, or even know about. But it must be beyond the call of duty; in fact, it must be *grossly* unfair to ask me to do it. It must be something I would naturally delay doing, something that I can't force myself to do without first obtaining the Holy Spirit. It can't be something I can do on my own.

It may be that I can't bless my enemy directly because of the intervening time or distance since the offense occurred. I might have lost contact with my former adversaries, and I may not even know how to locate them again. What if my enemy has died?

How can I obtain a healing miracle when I lack the chance to return good for evil?

In cases like these, there is still an offering I can make. I can offer assistance to my adversary's children or spouse. I can speak well of my enemy before others. I can assume that he has repented in the spirit world and imagine what he might say now about our conflict. I can always pray for my enemy. The Lord knows where he is, and I can always ask a blessing for him.

Jesus gave us a few case studies as our examples of how to do this:

"Ye have heard that it hath been said, An eye for an eye, and a tooth for a tooth: But I say unto you, That ye resist not evil: but whosoever shalt smite thee on thy right cheek, turn to him the other also. And if any man will sue thee at the law, and take away thy coat, let him have thy cloak also. And whosoever shall compel thee to go a mile, go with him twain" (Matthew 5:38–41).

It would be tempting to say that Jesus was exaggerating a little to make a point. Many prefer to think that Jesus used such poetic devices to teach a religion of peace, nonviolence, and passive resistance. That's a good philosophy, but it's not the gospel of Jesus Christ. The gospel is not a means of getting around the other guy, or of changing the other guy, or even of surviving until the other guy leaves. It is the means of growing toward the light, by living as Jesus lives, working as Jesus works, and loving as Jesus loves. It offers joy as its reward, a deep down sense of God's love so satisfying that many have given up their peaceful circumstances to obtain it.

I don't think the Lord was exaggerating in these case studies. Jesus first set the stage with a review of Mosaic tort law, which specified that someone found guilty of personal injury to another must suffer the same injury because of the inability to restore the function of the organ (eye or tooth) that was lost. Then the Lord announced that there was an even higher form of this law. Three examples of the application of this higher law are discussed below:

1. If my neighbor concludes a heated discussion by giving me a black eye, should I go back and talk to him again, possibly

giving him a chance to blacken my other eye as well? That really isn't what I feel like doing. Actually, I think I'd like a chance to administer the law of Moses and have him stand there while I take a good swing at his face.

But if I were allowed to do that, would my bad feelings go away? Once we were even, would I go back home and forget the whole thing? No, I think that for some time I would rehearse in my mind the injustice of his first punch, the less than Christlike satisfaction of my retribution, and the secret suspicion that one of us got in a better lick than the other one did. I might well hope for another chance to have it out together so I could beat him this time, fair and square.

So, what happens if I go to him and take a chance on having two black eyes? If I knew that by going back to his house I was offering a sacrifice on the Lord's altar, and if I felt the Savior's presence with me as I went there, I believe He would make up the difference to me in a feeling of joy. A joyous heart and a sore face. I can live with that sort of trade-off. Moreover, I might not be daydreaming later about a rematch.

2. But what if everyone thinks he's right and I'm wrong? What if he takes me to small-claims court and falsely claims that I tore a hole in his hunting jacket, when we both know he did it himself? What if the court finds in his favor, and I have to give him the new hunting jacket I got last Christmas? Am I supposed to throw in my poncho as well?

That's not what I want to do. I want to meticulously take out two of every three seams in my hunting jacket and enjoy the show as it falls apart on him. Let's see if his lying in court is going to do him any good. He can just forget any thought that I'm ever going to go hunting with him again! For that matter, I'm dropping out of his carpool; I'll walk before I ever get in the car with that guy again. It's a shame though. We used to be good friends. What if he repents and wants to apologize to me someday? If I slam the door on our friendship, we'll never have the chance to make things right again.

So, what happens if I do give him that poncho? In the first

place, the injustice of the whole thing would very nearly break my heart, and I would probably put if off for a while. In fact, I would never get around to it unless I suddenly felt inspired during a prayer, and I got up and went over to his house before I lost my nerve.

So, let's say I give him the poncho, and he accepts it in a confused sort of way ("Hey, what are you up to here?"). Then I go back home, and I think back on that court hearing of a few days before: Am I as angry and hurt now? I don't think I am. Some of that resentment has been swallowed up in the experience of giving him the poncho. In fact, I might get a better night's sleep than I have since I first got the court summons.

3. But what if it isn't my friend who has misused me but someone who has no regard for me at all? What if it's a soldier of an invading country who enjoys rubbing my face in it by insisting that I carry his gear for a certain distance, as the laws of his country allow? Maybe I'm running late already, and I don't have time for such nonsense. Am I really supposed to carry that backpack to the market, as the law insists I do and then stand by and offer to carry it back for him also? That second-mile would add insult to injury!

I'd rather die than do one thing more for my enemy than I absolutely must! As it is, I'm going to come home today in a very bad mood, and my wife, children, and dog are going to sense my mood. I'll bet they stay out of my way. I might feel a little better when I wake up tomorrow morning, but then I'll probably see some other soldier on the street corner, and my seething rage will come back to me in full force.

Perhaps I'll get a transfer to some faraway land where the Roman presence is minimal. It would be far from home, but it would be worth it to get away from those accursed Romans! What if I do go to such a place, and then when I'm an old man I come home for a visit and I see a young Roman soldier in the plaza. Won't my hatred spring back to life? Can I *ever* let it go?

Okay, what if I do what the Savior says, and I do stick around the market until he's finished shopping, and I go to him and ask if I can carry his stuff back to the fort? He may remind me that he can't force me to do it, and of course that's the whole point. It's a freewill offering I'm making, and I'm really making the offering to the Lord, not to him. Well, he may think I'm just a little stupid, or maybe somewhat awed by his military grandeur, but suppose he does let me carry his stuff back? How will I feel?

I'll get home a little later than otherwise, but I'll greet my wife, my kids, and my dog with a smile that reflects the miracle I experienced. I exercised my faith in the Lord and did the impossible. I couldn't take such a step without it taking some of the steam out of my grudge. My deep hatred for the whole Roman Empire was swallowed up, in part at least, when I held the Savior's hand and made my "second-mile offering."

FORGIVE ALL MEN

When I read the Savior's teachings, I ask myself, "What if He was serious? What if He actually meant what He was saying?" I realize it really is asking too much to insist that the victims should bless the offenders, but then the reward Jesus offers us is quite beyond what any of us could earn on our own either. Maybe the chief reason we live in a world with so much potential for pain is so we can experience the miracle of healing He offers us. Maybe life only makes sense when such a miracle is part of it.

I know intellectually that His atonement has swallowed up sin and suffering, but when adversity is upon me that seems so hard to remember, so immaterial to what I'm going through. But keeping this commandment brings it home. No one can bless his enemy under the influence of the Holy Spirit and not experience the healing miracle we're talking about.

We've read where the Lord declared this principle as the key to becoming "the children of your Father which is in heaven." He concluded the Sermon on the Mount with this additional admonition:

"Therefore whosoever heareth these sayings of mine, and doeth them, I will liken him unto a wise man, which built his house upon a rock: And the rain descended, and the floods came, and the winds blew, and beat upon that house; and it fell not: for it was founded upon a rock. And every one that heareth these sayings of mine, and doeth them not, shall be likened unto a foolish man, which built his house upon the sand: And the rain descended, and the floods came, and the winds blew, and beat upon that house; and it fell: and great was the fall of it" (Matthew 7:24–27).

The Lord was serious when He gave these doctrines. Take them away and you've taken away the greatest healing miracles. Take away these healing miracles and you no longer have a religion that can save you. I don't have to get well from a serious illness or injury in order to obtain exaltation. I don't have to overcome my fears before I can enter into the kingdom of heaven. Both would be nice, and both are possible, but neither is a condition of salvation. However, I do have to repent of my sins, and I have to forgive others, or I'm going to find myself standing on the outside looking in. No one can enter the kingdom of heaven while burdened with either unrepented sin or unforgiven grudges.

Jesus repeatedly paired repentance and forgiveness, and it's evident that these are two sides of the same coin. In the Lord's Prayer, Jesus said, "And forgive us our debts, as we forgive our debtors" (Matthew 6:12). Immediately following this prayer, He added, "For if ye forgive men their trespasses, your heavenly Father will also forgive you: But if ye forgive not men their trespasses, neither will your Father forgive your trespasses" (vv. 14–15).

In the early days of the Restoration, the Lord taught:

"Wherefore, I say unto you, that ye ought to forgive one another; for he that forgiveth not his brother his trespasses standeth condemned before the Lord; for there remaineth in him the greater sin. I, the Lord, will forgive whom I will forgive, but of you it is required to forgive all men" (D&C 64:9–10).

This is another hard doctrine, which tells us that there's probably a very special miracle concealed within it. I don't believe this scripture is designed to twist people's arms into saying, "I forgive you," just so everyone else can relax and consider the matter past. The point of everything we've said so far is that it has to be real. A miracle of healing has to occur to make it real, and we are required to seek this miracle, either in this world or in the world to come.

The Lord doesn't say how long it should take to realize this miracle. Thank heavens for that! We can't just forgive on our own; the Holy Spirit must empower us to make an offering, and who can say exactly when that will happen? There is a complex interplay of "my will" and "thy will" each time we receive a revelation from God, and sometimes it takes longer for this to happen for reasons we don't clearly understand.

When clients struggle with forgiveness issues, I teach them the principle of the second-mile offering, and I encourage them to put it into practice. Once they understand the principle, however, I leave it to them to apply it to their own situations. I never know how long it will be before the Spirit leads them to make a second-mile offering, so I don't push. Impatience or pressure from me is certainly not going to help anything. For some things, you just have to wait for a season of growth. But whether it comes sooner or later, I have seen this miracle too many times to doubt that the Lord's help is real and that He can heal us.

FORGIVING OUR ETERNAL COMPANIONS

How does this principle relate to temple marriage? In the last chapter, we noted that our hearts are most often injured by those closest to us, whether accidentally or on purpose. We also examined how fear can form a wall between spouses and how that wall can destroy the sense of oneness we all want so much. Unresolved resentment between spouses can form even thicker walls.

Guardrail: Gift to the Lord

I often hear an angry husband declare bitterly, "I know what would make her happy; she'd be tickled pink if I would . . ." Just

as often a wife will tearfully say, "Sure, he'd love it if I'd only
. . ." The one making the statement assumes that these demands
are obviously too unreasonable to be met and that no rational
person could expect such a concession. Generally there is also the
assumption that the offending spouse wants only what he or she
wants and would never consider offering what the grieved spouse
wants in return.

What these couples rarely realize is that they may have just
defined the second-mile offering that the Lord might ask of them.
Assuming their companion has a righteous request, wouldn't
the Lord be pleased with such a sacrifice? Perhaps they could
rephrase their sentences, saying, "I know what would make the
Lord happy; He'd be tickled pink if I would . . ." or "Sure, the
Lord would love it if I'd only . . ." Would this make a difference?
Many couples find they can only bless their spouses if they consider it a gift to the Lord. Doing so, in fact, constitutes another
guardrail for couples whose struggle with resentment impedes
their ability to keep their sealing covenant.

Sam and Lisa

Sam and Lisa had developed a fairly secure temple marriage,
at least until a job transfer brought them back into the neighborhood where Sam grew up. He'd always put his wife first while
they were living away, but Lisa noticed soon after the move that
Sam seemed to resent anything she said that differed from his
family's perspective. It wasn't long before she began to notice a
disapproving expression on his face when he would look at her,
and a new tone in his voice told her it was time for her to stop
making waves. Not only did Sam now sit back in an easy chair
and let his mother wait on him during visits home, but he seemed
less interested in spending time alone with Lisa. As far as Lisa
could tell, Sam had grown tired of adult life and had moved back
home.

Each time Lisa spoke to Sam about these feelings, a quarrel ensued. It seemed no matter how Lisa approached the subject, Sam would turn the conversation around where she had to

defend her way of doing things. This conflict soon colored every interaction they had. It wasn't long before the labeling began. No longer was Sam behaving childishly; now he was a mama's boy. No longer was Lisa feeling resentful; now she was disagreeable. News of their marital distress traveled swiftly among Sam's extended family, and his relatives sympathized with him about Lisa's attitude. She was clearly outnumbered!

What started out as hurt feelings quickly grew into soul-felt resentment, and physical intimacy ended between them. Sam chalked it up to a bad attitude getting worse. Lisa saw it as a wake-up call and wondered why Sam was ignoring it. They began to argue less often, but then they rarely talked at all. Sam finally suggested that they should consider marriage counseling.

During the first therapy sessions, we established that Sam and Lisa had once loved each other and that there was a time when they had been optimistic about the future. But since their estrangement, they felt lonely, abandoned, and vulnerable to the attentions of other men and women. Fortunately, neither seemed likely to have an affair anytime soon. Their religious faith was still too strong for that.

Tears came to Sam and Lisa as they described their disappointment. How could Lisa be married to a man who refused to stand up for her and show the world he cherished her? How could Sam live with a woman who would throw a fit each time she didn't get her own way? Sam and Lisa were trying to understand what had gone wrong, and with some assistance, they were able to express each other's point of view. But that was where therapy foundered. It was obvious that engineering a compromise would not address their pain. The question at hand had become, "Even if my partner did give in a little, do I want this marriage anymore?" They were tired and discouraged. They both felt that the other could have avoided all this but didn't choose to.

Lisa made the first second-mile offering, although Sam didn't know it at the time. Lisa prayed sincerely to know what she could do to get the beam out of her own eye, and she felt inspired to find something about her mother-in-law that she could compliment. Her first attempt was a real fiasco. No sooner had they arrived at his parents' house than her father-in-law started criticizing her children's behavior, and Lisa left with the kids as soon as she could manage it.

Lisa's next attempt was better. She mentioned to her mother-in-law that Sam had obviously had a secure childhood. Even as she said this, Lisa realized that she really was grateful that Sam had grown up in a loving and nurturing home. Lisa felt the Spirit confirm to her that she had harvested much that Sam's parents had sown. It was becoming clearer to Lisa that her own heart was beginning to soften.

Although they were never sure whose idea it was, Lisa and Sam made love that night for the first time in several months. The next day, Sam commented about the possibility of relocating again, and he wondered why this should surprise Lisa. Surely she didn't think he was going to stay with his present job forever! Something was changing.

The changes came slowly, however. It even seemed that things were getting worse at first because Sam and Lisa began quarreling at the same time they began talking again. They remained living in the same town, and visits with Sam's family were still uncomfortable for Lisa. But her ability to let comments slide had grown, and Lisa no longer found herself rehearsing unkind remarks for days afterward.

Then after a rather mundane disagreement with her mother-in-law, Sam gently suggested to his mother that he agreed with Lisa this time. The issue was not very important, but Sam's loyal support was extremely important to Lisa. It was later that she learned that Sam was also making a second-mile offering.

After they both realized that the war was over, Sam and Lisa were able to talk about what had happened. Rather than worrying about who was most to blame for their conflict, they focused on how they had applied their marriage covenant and how much richer their relationship was now.

Lisa had blessed Sam by being tolerant with his family, and Sam had blessed Lisa by standing up for her. Because of the grudge that was lodged in their hearts, neither of them had felt their spouse deserved the blessing, but both made the offering because of their covenant with the Lord.

The conflict did not just go away, nor would this be the last disagreement in their marriage. However, Sam and Lisa were a couple again, receiving one another in the new and everlasting covenant of marriage. They had put it on the Lord's account. The price was paid.

This case was one where both spouses had offended each other. Would anything be different if only one of the spouses had injured the other? What about a case of adultery? Jesus disapproved of divorce "except it be for fornication" (Matthew 19:9), so isn't adultery something of an unforgivable sin in marriage? I don't think it has to be.

George and Darla

George and Darla enjoyed spending time with Glen and Marie. The two couples had attended the same ward, had worked together in church callings, and had even gone on temple trips together. They had been best friends for several years when Darla and Glen began to have feelings for one another, and they had a brief affair.

Almost immediately, the attraction they felt for each other vanished as they began to appreciate how much they had lost in their adventure. Knowing they would likely lose both their marriages and their Church membership, they agreed that neither would ever tell anyone else what had happened between them. Eventually, Glen and Marie moved away, and the two couples rarely saw each other anymore.

A few years later, however, Darla felt she could no longer live with herself. She knew she was taking the sacrament unworthily, and it was becoming obvious that she was just making excuses to avoid attending the temple. Darla confessed her sin to her bishop, and a few weeks later, she was disfellowshipped in a disciplinary council. She let Glen know she had made this confession, and he resolved to do the same thing. Glen decided to wait a while longer to make his confession, however, so no one would link his disciplinary council with Darla's, and Marie would never know that Darla was the other woman.

Darla felt it her duty to confess to George as well, but she could not bring herself to tell him that Glen had betrayed him also. Darla told George that the affair was entirely over and that there was no need for her to identify her lover to anyone other than the bishop. George took some of the blame for the rift that had preceded her affair, and he told Darla that he felt some relief at finally identifying what had stood between them. George was able to tell Darla that evening that he could forgive her for her infidelity and that they could set about to rebuild their temple marriage.

Within a few days, however, they both realized that such promises are easier to make than to keep. Every conversation seemed to swing around to the topic of the affair. George repeatedly asked Darla to tell him who the other man was, and he wanted to know details about how they had met, what they had actually done together, and whether she had been in love with him. When it became apparent that Darla had already told him all she was ever going to say, George became very resentful and suspicious of nearly every man around them.

While Darla had felt significant relief after confessing her sin to her bishop, she now felt that her guilt would never go away. She was tempted to tell George everything and get it over with, but she was sure his pain (and anger) would only escalate if she did so. However, Darla knew she couldn't live with this black cloud hovering over their home, and she began to consider a separation. She suggested counseling to George, and he enthusiastically agreed, obviously hoping that the therapist would help Darla understand that she owed it to her husband to answer his questions.

They were a very likable couple, and I truly hoped they could salvage their temple marriage. George was disappointed when I told him I couldn't encourage his wife to make a full disclosure to him, but he did seem grateful to have someone with whom he could vent his feelings safely. George knew he was becoming obsessed with his questions, and he also knew it was affecting his love for Darla. There was never any question that George wanted to forgive her, but it was proving to be much harder than he had imagined. He began to be tempted to also have an affair, but he knew this would only serve to get even with Darla, to make her hurt the way he was hurting.

We had been meeting for several weeks when I first discussed with George how he might begin to feel better if he made a second-mile offering. As always happens when someone first hears this principle, George was struck with how unfair it was that he should have to be the one to make the first sacrifice. After all, Darla was the one who betrayed him. Why shouldn't she be the one to make it up to him?

Eventually, George recognized that he was the one with the wound, and he began to prayerfully consider what he could do that would soften his own heart. George came to the conclusion that he should submit himself to his bishop, who, as the presiding high priest, was authorized to receive such answers by revelation. The bishop prayed about George's question and counseled him to give Darla a priesthood blessing as a comfort to her during the time her church activity was restricted. The moment he received this inspired direction, George realized that he didn't want to do it, which is a sure sign that the bishop had identified the correct second-mile offering.

George had promised the bishop that he would give Darla the blessing right away, but days passed and he had not yet brought himself to do it. He felt bad for having such a hard heart, and he began to sincerely pray for the Lord to nudge him into action. George never felt any particular answer to that prayer, but finally the moment came when he asked Darla if she would like a priesthood blessing, and she accepted his offer without delay.

George told me that he received considerably more comfort from that blessing than Darla did. During the next few days, he found himself marveling at how much he loved her, amazed by his good fortune that Darla loved him in return. The affair began to shrink in importance until it finally became only one link in an unfortunate chain of events. George would never forget what had happened, but he did begin to forget the pain associated with it. He began to heal. Darla still didn't tell him at that time that his close friend was the other man, but George felt much more prepared to wait until she felt right about telling him.

Couples with grieved hearts will not be able to receive each other until their wounds are healed by the Savior's touch. Those who brood over injustices are trapped, estranged from God's love as much as from their spouse's love. If repentance requires a miracle, so does the ability to forgive others. But there is a way out of the trap. Jesus has told us how. We can realize this miracle when we bless our enemy by making a second-mile offering to the Lord.

THE BEST DEFENSE

Is there ever a time when it's okay to retaliate? Is there such a thing as righteous anger? When can we say, "Enough is enough. Leave me alone or I'll make you wish you had!"

I remember one Saturday afternoon when my then four-year-old son came to join me as I worked in the garden. "Dad," he began, "what if there was a big ugly monster in our yard? What would you do?"

"Why, I'd ask him to leave," I replied.

"But what if he wouldn't leave? What would you do?"

"I'd tell him he had to leave."

"But what if he was really ugly and scary, and he wouldn't leave?" By now, he was getting a little frustrated with my pacifism. "What if he was going to hurt us?"

"Well," I said, "I would just tell him that he had to leave, right now . . ." The poor boy was almost crying. "Or else!" I added.

"Yes!" he exclaimed. "*Or else!*" He brightened considerably. "Or else what, Dad?"

Finally, I was saying something that made sense. He wasn't going to relax until he knew I was going to punch that monster out and send him away from our house. But is this ever the correct solution to conflict? From the themes addressed so far, it might appear that such is never the case. However, part of the scriptural message is that God sends His children forth with both blessings and punishments.

There is a difference, however, between license and authority. This isn't a case of "Do whatever you want, and I'll back you up later." Rather, those who represent God must lay aside their own desires and wishes and submit themselves to the will of God.

When a priesthood holder blesses the sick, he can't declare an instant blessing simply because that's what he wants. As he lays his hands upon the head of the one afflicted, he must be equally prepared to pronounce a blessing of comfort amidst ongoing trials, if that's what the Spirit moves him to say. In like manner, God isn't going to use one of His children to punish another of His children simply to get even. We can't come representing ourselves; we must come representing God.

"Dearly beloved, avenge not yourselves, but rather give place unto wrath: for it is written, Vengeance is mine; I will repay, saith the Lord" (Romans 12:19).

The only circumstance where we can fight back and have the Lord's approval is when we have already overcome our need to get even, when our only motivation is to do God's will. The Lord gave very specific instructions concerning this principle in D&C 98, at a time when the Latter-day Saints had every reason to retaliate against mobbers who had killed some, beaten many, and driven all the rest from their homes.

"Now, I speak unto you concerning your families—if men will smite you, or your families, once, and ye bear it patiently and revile not against them, neither seek revenge, ye shall be rewarded; but if ye bear it not patiently, it shall be accounted unto you as being meted out as a just measure unto you" (vv. 23–24).

The Lord is saying that if we hit back, we're on our own. Our standing is equal before the Lord. "Kids, I don't care who started it," He might say. Christians must sacrifice the reflex to retaliate. Even when we have the clout to make our enemies back off, we can't indulge in doing so without sacrificing our standing as Christians. That's where long-suffering comes in.

"And again, if your enemy shall smite you the second time, and you revile not against your enemy, and bear it patiently, your reward shall be an hundredfold. And again, if he shall smite you the third time, and ye bear it patiently, your reward shall be doubled unto you four-fold; and these three testimonies shall stand against your enemy if he repent not, and shall not be blotted out. . . . I have delivered thine enemy into thine hands . . . and if thou rewardest him according to his works thou art justified" (vv. 25–31).

Children of Christ cannot punish their enemies in the name and strength of the Lord unless they've first cleansed their hearts of the spirit of revenge. They must first remove the beam from their eyes with a second-mile offering to the Lord by forbearing to retaliate until they lose the desire to get even. That's much easier said than done. To receive unjustified blows without retaliation is a painful and humbling experience. However, only when we have subjugated our will to the will of the Father can we go forth in the name of the Lord and count on Him to fight our battles.

Verses 33–38 go on to explain that this law applies to nations as well as individuals. It also applies to conflicts between parents and children, and it applies to conflicts between spouses. Sometimes a man's foes are those of his own household. However, children of Christ should never feel satisfaction when repeated offenses justify finally taking action. Rather, there should be a heartfelt sympathy for anyone who merits divine censure.

Wayne and Cindy

Wayne reluctantly agreed to be the noncustodial parent in his divorce with Cindy on the premise that the children needed a mother at home. But things had changed since then. Wayne had joined the Church, and he took every opportunity to share his new faith with his children. Furthermore, Wayne had been blessed a year later to have a temple marriage with a woman who seemed to love his children. And now he wanted so much to have his children sealed to him.

Then he learned that Cindy's new husband was being transferred to another state, and Wayne was really upset. Why should he be further separated from his children when she was the one electing to move? When Wayne learned that Cindy's move would also require the children to be latchkey kids while their mother worked, he decided that the time had come to make his move.

His attorney told him that a court hearing at this time would likely result in Wayne's receiving custody, and he advised Wayne to seize the opportunity. Wayne spoke with relatives in order to consolidate a consensus of support for this decision, and he also spoke with his bishop.

The bishop reminded Wayne that such a big decision requires more than human wisdom, and he asked Wayne to sincerely seek God's will in this matter. Wayne agreed to fast and pray before beginning legal proceedings, but he really couldn't imagine why the Lord would frown on the decision he'd already made. Wayne felt he'd been wronged in the first place, and now it was time for things to go his way.

During the following week, however, Wayne began to experience nagging doubts about his plan. He couldn't dispel from his mind how much this was going to hurt Cindy. Finally, Wayne phoned Cindy and told her about his desire for custody and asked her if she would agree to it without a court battle. Her response to this fair play gesture was to file first, seeking supervised visitation on the basis of false allegations.

Wayne was crushed! He began to doubt the inspiration he'd received. He admitted to his attorney that he'd been wrong to tip his hand that way, but his attorney reassured him that he'd still win in the end. However, Wayne had to promise that he wouldn't do anything else to jeopardize their case. His attorney told him that the time had come to play to win.

Then Wayne began to experience more whisperings of the Spirit. He realized that the Lord wasn't just concerned with who would win in court; He cared most about Wayne's spiritual state.

Wayne barely had the courage to admit to his attorney that he was allowing Cindy to take the kids with her on a house-hunting trip on his weekend. His attorney asked if Wayne was out of his mind.

Wayne hoped that Cindy would follow his lead and retract her allegations, and he prayed she'd finally decide to let him have custody without the rancor of a court battle. She didn't. In fact, Cindy used the extra time Wayne had given her to introduce doubts into the children's minds about their father's conduct. Once again, Wayne wondered where the Lord's hand was in all this.

As it turned out, Wayne lost the case. Cindy dropped the allegations from a lack of evidence, but she won the right to take the children out of state anyway. Wayne had the opportunity during the final hearing to malign Cindy's character the way she had slandered his, but he just couldn't do it. He no longer wanted to get even, and for the third time, he chose to turn the other cheek.

However, two years later the children independently decided they wanted to live with their father. They were so insistent that Cindy eventually consented. Wayne now pays all expenses for the children to visit their mother, and he encourages them to love and respect her. Both children joined the Church soon after coming to live with their father, and Wayne is proud of the fine young people they've turned out to be.

Wayne knows he probably would've won custody of the children right away if he'd followed his attorney's advice. However, he also knows that doing so might have won him the battle but cost him the war. Wayne shudders to think of the outcome if he had used no more than mortal wisdom and strength. His children might have so resented the bloody battle they would have been forced to witness that they may well have pushed away from both parents!

Wayne could have hit back, but he didn't. Instead, he made a series of second-mile offerings and overcame the desire for revenge. Had the Lord then directed him to fight back, Wayne would no longer have felt any satisfaction in the mission. Perhaps that's why it's so rare for the Lord to use victims to bring aggressors to justice. In the end, Cindy gave up with no further fight. The Lord Himself brought peace to the battlefield.

I'm not pretending that this treatment for grieved hearts is either simple or painless, but I have found that it works every time. If we do what Christ has asked us to do, He can heal us once, seven times, or seventy times seven times. The power of this healing comes from deep in the Garden of Gethsemane and the pain that Jesus suffered for us there. He has invited us to put our pain, our resentment, our sense of injustice, and our desire for revenge on His account. It's paid for.

Wherefore, the Lord God gave unto man that he should act for himself. Wherefore, man could not act for himself save it should be that he was enticed by the one or the other.
—2 Nephi 2:16

CHAPTER FIVE

ENTICED BY THE ONE OR THE OTHER

Father Lehi was the preeminent visionary of the Book of Mormon, having founded both the race and the worldview of that great civilization. There is simple grandeur in his tree of life vision, and each of us can easily find our life's position somewhere in the scene that Lehi describes. One of us is lost in the mists of darkness, another is clutching the iron rod for dear life, and another clearly sees both the great and spacious building and the tree with its delicious white fruit. And that last man has a choice.

The power to choose, which we call agency, is the thread that runs throughout all of Lehi's teachings, and it is the foundation of the Nephite's religion. We don't have the record of everything

Lehi taught, but we do have Nephi's account of his father's final words of blessing and direction to his family, and this is where we get the chance to really understand what Lehi knew about agency.

When it came time to bless his fifth son, Jacob, Lehi launched into an ambitious examination of why the world is as it is. He explained to Jacob why the Lord has affixed both rewards and punishments and why He has given them roughly equal magnitudes: "For it must needs be, that there is an opposition in all things. If not so, my first-born in the wilderness, righteousness could not be brought to pass, neither wickedness, neither holiness nor misery, neither good nor bad. Wherefore, all things must needs be a compound in one . . . wherefore there would have been no purpose in the end of its creation" (2 Nephi 2:11–12).

What if there had been no options to choose from? What if God had never given commandments? If that had been the case, there would have been no difference between right and wrong, and life would have had no meaning. No one could have hoped for anything greater than peace and pleasure, because joy is only experienced as we reach painfully beyond peace and pleasure. Yet Lehi declared that "men are, that they might have joy" (2 Nephi 2:25). He prophesied of the Atonement and explained that this atonement would give us extra time for our test so that we can mature in how we make choices before we are judged for those choices.

Then Lehi gave Jacob the answer to one of the most perplexing religious questions of all time: Why does there have to be a devil, and what could possibly be in it for him? If God didn't want men to sin, then why did he cast Satan down to earth? Why didn't He send Satan straight to hell in the first place?

"Wherefore, men are free according to the flesh; and all things are given them which are expedient unto man. And they are free to choose liberty and eternal life, through the great Mediator of all men, or to choose captivity and death, according to the captivity and power of the devil; for he seeketh that all men might be miserable like unto himself" (2 Nephi 2:27).

Lehi taught that God urges us to make the right choices because He wants us to have joy. However, if God had been the only one to prompt us in this way, our agency would have been compromised. Surely we would have been so awed by His presence as to obey His will to the letter, regardless of how we might otherwise have chosen. Therefore, Satan was sent here because "man could not act for himself save it should be that he was enticed by the one or the other" (2 Nephi 2:16). Prompted by both God and Satan, we can use our agency to cast the deciding vote. That is how God gave man his agency, as well as the freedom to exercise it.

There are actually four options we can choose from:

1. We can choose to keep our covenants with God.
2. We can choose to ignore these covenants.
3. We can choose to break these covenants.
4. We can choose to form a covenant with Satan.

Whether we make our covenants in mortality or in the spirit world, each of us who has ever lived is going to anchor his soul to one of these four choices. How we choose will reveal the sort of person we are. How we choose will determine our eternal reward.

Those who choose to keep their covenants will have joy in the celestial kingdom; all others will have something less than that. Because God desires all His children to inherit the celestial kingdom, He will give all of us the same invitation—to reach to Him for the power to keep our covenants. Satan, however, will try to convince us that only the three lower choices are possible, and he wins at least a partial victory anytime we settle for less than a celestial glory!

When we are baptized, we covenant to live as Jesus lives. Those who keep that covenant are the ones who strive to obey the Lord's commandments, even when they must sacrifice to do so. Those who ignore that covenant are the ones who pick and choose the commandments they will keep. Those who break that covenant are the ones who build a lifestyle of sin, who define themselves by the sins they choose. Finally, those who covenant with Satan are the ones who would seek out the covenant keepers in order to corrupt them.

When we are endowed, we covenant to work as Jesus works. Those who keep that covenant are the ones who magnify their callings with the power of the Holy Ghost, who enjoy revelations, miracles, and gifts of the Spirit in their labors. Those who ignore that covenant are the ones who fill callings without power and bury their talent. Those who break this covenant are the ones who drop out of the race, not even lending their presence to the work of the kingdom. Finally, those who covenant with Satan are the apostates who are just as dedicated to fighting the Savior's work as true disciples are in promoting it.

Not surprisingly, we also find these four choices among those who have been sealed as spouses. Those who keep this covenant are the ones who love as Jesus loves as they receive their partners in the new and everlasting covenant they have with the Lord. Those who ignore this covenant are the ones who conduct a temple marriage exactly as though it were a civil marriage, basing their life together merely on principles of fairness and reciprocity. Those who break this covenant are the ones who emotionally reject their spouses, usually because of fear, resentment, or competing attractions. Lastly, those who covenant with Satan are the ones who, having themselves turned away from God, now seek to separate their spouses from God as well.

Many people initially choose to keep their covenants but then become discouraged and settle for less. We examined in the last two chapters what we can do if fear or resentment prevents us from keeping the covenant to love our spouses as Jesus loves us. The present chapter examines what someone can do if he's not keeping this covenant because he is enticed away by some other competing attraction.

PUTTING OUR MARRIAGES FIRST

We typically think of "the other woman" when we discuss competing attractions, but there are many other possible competitors for our devotion. Many men and women have turned from their temple marriages to pursue fame and fortune, hobbies and amusements, relationships with family and friends, service in the Church and community, and, of course, appetites and pleasures.

There is nothing wrong with any of these things. In fact, our lives would be fairly imbalanced if we did not make room for each of these competing attractions. The problem arises when we supplant our marriages with one of these things. It may be difficult to recognize the first symptoms of such infidelity, but we can discern by the Holy Spirit when our investment in some new person or activity is accompanied by a corresponding dis-investment in our marriages.

The first signs of such disloyalty can be very subtle. The husband begins to work longer hours at work so the family can afford the new addition to their home. The wife takes a late afternoon college class because that's the only time the course is offered. He finds himself constantly thinking about the problems of families in the ward since being called to be an elders quorum president. She has waited so long to be a mother that she wants to be near her baby day and night.

None of these things is wrong or evil. Many couples with healthy temple marriages make such adjustments in their schedules all the time. There is no problem unless our new investment of interest and energy is accompanied by a decrease in our feelings toward our eternal mate. However, if we do notice some emotional distance in that relationship, we probably should be a little concerned, especially if we begin to begrudge the time and energy that our marriage requires.

There is no one among us who has been married for any length of time who has not had at least one competing interest. It may not necessarily have been a physical attraction for another person, but there will be something outside of the marriage that threatens to steal some of the feeling between the couple.

We must take this threat seriously. If I deny the fact that I can easily fall into this trap, then I won't be aware of the danger until it's too late. Before I know it, my sweetheart is going to feel insecure, no longer sure that I'm there to receive her anymore. If

I'm not careful, I may become less sure of that myself.

The danger begins with one of those harmless and unavoidable shifts in how I allocate my personal time and energy. If I'm honest with myself, and I do find that something has grown more important to me than my marriage, then I must accept the fact that I'm being enticed by a competing interest. If the situation presents a significant challenge to my marriage, it may be wisest for me to eliminate the competing interest. I might work fewer hours, drop out of the class, ask for a release, or use a babysitter.

However, if I choose to preserve my marriage without making such a change, then I must begin immediately to reinvest in my relationship with my spouse. It's not necessary that I devote the same amount of time doing this as my new competing interest requires; I can't create more hours in a day. But when I find that I've overdrawn my marriage account, I must immediately add something to it again. I must put down what I'm doing and deliberately begin some new activity with my eternal mate. It might be putting in a garden together, or folding the clothes together, or taking walks in the evening, or even involving her in my new competing activity—but it has to be something I wasn't doing before.

This new activity will help to restore our union. But more important, this will be an offering on the Lord's altar, a call for help requesting that He touch my heart and restore the feelings I'm losing. It will be following Mormon's invitation to "pray unto the Father with all the energy of heart, that ye may be filled with this love" (Moroni 7:48).

We're not discussing here the due that we owe our spouses or that they owe us. The problem is not how we treat each other, but how our hearts work. If my heart is losing its feeling for my spouse, it has nothing to do with whether she is treating me well. The problem is with my heart. I'm the one who needs healing, and I'm the one who must ask the Lord for a healing miracle.

Another second-mile offering is needed. If I ask in sincere prayer, the Spirit will inspire me to know what feelings I should express, what concession I should make, or what activity I should share that will bring about the renewal of my love. Jesus taught, "For where your treasure is, there will your heart be also" (Matthew 6:21). This simple formula is a promise. As I devote new energy to my marriage, my heart will follow that lead, and my feelings can be rekindled.

This solution to a distracted heart may seem simplistic, yet relying on God's promises has always seemed to be too easily said to be easily done. However, He either keeps His promises or He doesn't, and I join many others in testifying that He does keep His promises.

When I was called to be a bishop a few years ago, my counselors and I found ourselves working around the clock for several months to organize a new ward, and it seemed that every spare waking moment was spent in driving, phoning, planning, meeting, or interviewing. It was without question the spiritual highlight of my life, and I treasure the special companionship I felt with the Savior in that calling. But I must confess that my family was relegated to "if-I-ever-get-around-to-it" status. Clearly, I was being enticed by a competing interest.

My wife was supportive, and she rapidly took over many of my family responsibilities so I could be the father of the ward. Date night went out the window. Quality time with my wife became conversations in the car if we were going to a meeting at the same time. I knew this wasn't good for my marriage, but I couldn't see other options, so we settled down for the duration. We were sure we'd survive as a couple, and we knew we'd someday look back on this period with deep satisfaction.

However, every time I thought to the future, I would feel a sense of loss. Something was slipping away from us. My relationship with my wife was cooling. When we saw each other at night, we would promptly run down our respective to-do lists to make sure that everything got done, and I found myself looking upon her more as a coworker than as a sweetheart. When I did spend time with her, I found I couldn't enjoy it; I was just catching my breath so I could go back to the bishop's office.

I had a number of friends, including my home teacher, our stake president, and most of our ward officers, who did everything possible to share some of my load, but this did not have much effect upon my marriage. I was surprised that even when I was able to free up some time, it made little difference. I began to see that my problem was more than a demanding schedule. My problem was that I loved the ward more than I loved my wife. I would never have admitted this was so, but look at who I made time for.

Things began to improve after I'd served for about one year, although my wife and I were not sure at first what had changed. It seemed perhaps that we had simply grown accustomed to the pace, but I remember writing in my journal that the pace had grown even worse! Something else had entered our lives that was restoring our sense of togetherness again. We were receiving one another as we had before.

As we look back, we see now that the turning point for us came when we took our family vacation that year. We almost didn't go. I hadn't been sure I could break away from work and Church responsibilities—and I wasn't sure I wanted to. A number of the families in the ward were in crisis, especially a member with a life-threatening health problem, and it seemed an unjustifiable indulgence to take off like that. However, I could tell that my wife needed us to spend time alone as a family again, and at the last minute, I decided to go.

For two weeks, I was a husband and father again. Taking time to talk with my wife was again a joy and not merely a lull in the work. She was more than a real support; she was my wife, and it mattered to me what was going on in her life. What's more, I didn't want to be on the back burner of her life until I was finally released.

Until that vacation, I had thought the problem was time. After that, I realized that the problem was love. I had been praying for time, but I never did get more than my twenty-four-hour-a-day allotment. On the other hand, while I had never actually prayed for love, I see now that bringing my family on that vacation served as my second-mile offering because I did receive an extra portion of love, just as Mormon said would happen. It had the feel of a miracle, and I believe this is what it was—a gift from Gethsemane to help me choose wisely.

But are there some responsibilities that must take precedence over our marriages? What about a sick or wayward child? Shouldn't the grown-ups be able to suspend their married life during such a crisis?

Nathan and Lori

Nathan and Lori had always worried about their sixteen-year-old daughter, Kristen, because she never seemed to worry about anything. Her grades were barely passing, her room was a mess, and she wasn't active in seminary. She didn't even seem to care very much about upcoming milestones like getting a job or taking driving lessons. It seemed the more anxious they were about upcoming tests, the less inclined Kristen was to study. The more determined they were to read scriptures as a family, the less agreeable she was to join in.

Nathan began to worry that his daughter might have to go to summer school if she didn't take her grades more seriously, and he developed a study calendar to help her get organized. He was irritated to learn that she didn't even know the dates of upcoming exams, and he insisted she get that information from each teacher.

Lori worried more that Kristen had begun to narrow her choice of friends to low achievers who were less active in the Church. She recognized the signal that her daughter's appearance and attitude was sending to other youth, and she began to nag Kristen about her posture, tone of voice, and "that look in her eyes."

Nathan and Lori never noticed when their concern for their daughter began to dominate every conversation or when they stopped looking forward to being alone together. They still had couple prayer each evening before bed, but even this brought them no sense of closeness. Sometimes they realized late in the night that they were both awake—but when they talked about their feelings, they struggled with the temptation to affix blame. Had Nathan been too controlling? Had Lori been too indulgent?

Lori was the first to make a second-mile offering. She humbled herself enough to sincerely ask Heavenly Father if she and Nathan were perhaps contributing to the problem. As she prayed, she suddenly recognized that the more they assumed the job of managing Kristen's life, the more Kristen would unconsciously relax in the certain knowledge that her parents were taking care of everything. Heavenly Father revealed to Lori that Kristen would become more responsible as soon as it became *her job* to worry about the outcome of her daily decisions.

Guardrail: Treats, Not Bailouts

In the meantime, Lori and Nathan would have to change their strategy. The Lord directed them to begin using a new guardrail, which was to give Kristen treats instead of bailouts. Anytime they found themselves worrying more about Kristen's responsibilities than she did, they needed to come together in prayer and ask for inspiration. They needed to agree on something they could do for Kristen that would show how much they loved her but that would not add to or diminish from the consequences of Kristen's own decisions.

Lori shared her newfound perspective with her husband, and Nathan was the first to recognize the benefit this new strategy would have on their marriage. For the first time in months, they would be on the same team again, coming to the Lord in heartfelt prayer together to identify the next treat and then throwing themselves into whatever labor was involved in bringing about the treat. Finally, instead of anguishing separately over each disappointment, they could now rejoice together in each new evidence of Kristen's growing maturity.

There were setbacks, of course. Old habits are hard to break. But each time Nathan and Lori resisted the urge to take over and each time they prepared another treat instead, they were making a second-mile offering to the Lord and were "filled with this love" that Mormon spoke of. It became another gift from Heavenly Father to two of His children—another gift from Gethsemane.

JUDGE NOT

There may also be occasions when we deliberately choose to close our hearts to each other. Sometimes we believe our spouses do not deserve our love. Perhaps we feel they are weaker than we thought them to be when we were first married. We may find that it has grown difficult to tolerate weaknesses and foibles in our partners that we would never tolerate in ourselves. It's hard to love someone you can't respect.

This is a common complaint of many of the couples who come in for counseling. I'm not sure how we all do it, but somehow most of us manage to find eternal mates who have gifts where we have weaknesses. Logically, this should make for a resilient marriage since, between the two of us, we should be able to do anything!

More often, however, we assume that our partner's weaknesses are more easily overcome than our own. We conclude that they must not love us very much if they won't make the slight effort needed to overcome them, even though it would make such a difference to us. Now, our own weaknesses are quite another matter. They would truly be difficult to overcome! In fact, if our spouses expect us to change something so obviously unchangeable, then that also proves they don't love us enough.

Naturally, the couples who come for counseling don't present their case in such a ludicrous manner. Usually it's a very serious discussion, often accompanied by tears or recriminations. However, when all is said and done, their positions typically boil down to those presented above. And the sad reality is that, no longer one flesh, they are once again alone.

I often review some pertinent scriptures with these couples, such as D&C 46:11, "To every man is given a gift by the Spirit of God," and Ether 12:27, "And if men come unto me I will show unto them their weakness. I give unto men weakness that they may be humble; and my grace is sufficient for all men that humble themselves before me; for if they humble themselves before me, and have faith in me, then will I make weak things become strong unto them."

Both strengths and weaknesses come from God, and we each seem to get our fair share of both upon entering mortality.

I don't see anything in these verses that says that strengths and weaknesses are only temporary. Some people read that last scripture to say, "If they humble themselves, then will I give them a gift to replace their weakness." That isn't how I read it. To me, it seems more reasonable for the Lord to say, "If they humble themselves, then will I help them do what they have to do—despite the fact that they're still weak in that area." The short boy is given a boost so he can see over the fence; he hasn't grown any, but he is able to see over the fence and that was all he needed. The Lord may compensate for our shortcomings, but He will rarely remove them.

Too often, we give our spouses the ultimatum, "I won't receive you until you change for me" (until you eliminate a weakness). I can't love someone who is disorganized, or nonassertive, or domineering. I'm not that way, so why are you that way? Of course, there's my personal favorite: "I can't love someone who is so needy." If my love is so important to you, then you can't have it!

Intolerance for our companion's weakness is another example of a competing attraction. In this case, we reject our spouse while receiving the person our spouse might have been. Who can compete with a fantasy person? The fantasy will win out every time. But this isn't the biggest problem; the problem is that we're refusing to receive our partner as we covenanted to do. The spouse is left out in the cold, rejected by the one who was supposed to love him as Jesus does.

If we find we are making this mistake, it's imperative that we make a second-mile offering at the Lord's altar as soon as possible. We need to petition the Savior to help us recover our love and appreciation for our eternal mate—by doing something so beyond the call of duty that we'll have to reach deeply into our souls to do it. These promises are real. The Lord will heal our hearts as soon as we admit to ourselves that this is what we need.

When we recover the feelings that were fading, we need to strengthen one another. We were given reciprocal strengths and weaknesses; why not step forward to help in those areas where we are strong and appreciate the spouse who steps forward in those areas where we are weak? Perhaps one of you finds it easier to say, "I'm sorry," yet the other one is better at saying, "Thank you." Maybe one of you is more patient with delays, but the other one has the endurance to stick with projects until they are finished. Perhaps one has a greater gift of communication, while the other has a knack for organization. Why not capitalize on our strengths instead of bellyaching about our weaknesses? The scriptures say that every one of us has at least one gift and at least one weakness, so who of us is better than his partner?

Dennis and Ann

Dennis and Ann's temple marriage was severely threatened by Dennis's reluctance to give priesthood blessings. From time to time, Ann would ask him to give her a blessing, yet Dennis never seemed willing to give one on the spur of the moment. He would ask her for a day or two to prepare but would never bring the subject up again. Ann began to see this pattern as evidence that Dennis didn't have a testimony or that he must not love her very much. In any event, Ann became blind to Dennis's other virtues, and she wished she'd married someone she could look up to as a worthy priesthood holder in the home.

For his part, Dennis was acutely aware that he didn't enjoy Ann's respect and used this to justify his timidity in priesthood matters. Dennis knew he had a testimony and had felt the Spirit on occasion, but he always shied away from situations where he would have to come through spiritually.

The more Ann pressured him, the more Dennis got even with her by pretending disinterest in priesthood activities. He began to leave other matters up to her also, such as calling the family together for prayer or presiding in family home evening. If all Ann wanted was priesthood on tap, with no concern for the performance pressure he felt, then Ann would just have to go get her blessings someplace else!

Their bishop noticed the growing stress in their relationship, and he referred Dennis and Ann for marriage counseling. In our first session, they quickly got to the point. Ann told Dennis that she felt he'd spiritually abandoned her. Dennis replied that he felt Ann didn't accept him for who he was. As often happens, the instant they both saw things from their partner's point of view, they were each seized by a sense of discouragement, a feeling that they might as well stop trying. After all, if it weren't this, it would just be something else!

This is a good time for a counselor to take a moment to teach true principles. This is the period of quiet when everyone takes stock of what has happened so far, and the clients are glad to take a break from their wrestling match. I noted that Dennis was having problems keeping his endowment covenant and that Ann was having problems keeping her sealing covenant. Neither of them had looked at their difficulties in that light before.

We talked about what they could do about it. Dennis and Ann could both see that their hearts were not right and that they must call down a healing blessing by making a pertinent offering. What was harder for them to understand, however, was the nature of that offering. What offering would touch their souls deeply? They left that first session feeling that something significant had been discussed, yet they were uncertain as to what would come next.

What did come next was that Dennis elected to say family prayer again. In fact, he didn't call on anyone else to say the prayer for nearly a week, but offered the prayer himself each time. Ann suspected he was just giving in and then going overboard to rub it in. But in reality, Dennis was practicing how to speak under inspiration. Actually, he wasn't thinking about Ann at all during that time; for once, Dennis was stretching himself spiritually, not because of Ann, but in spite of her. He really did want to keep his endowment covenant, and he was finally working to overcome his fear of failure.

Ann wasn't seeing this. All she could see was that Dennis was giving in to her, but not in the one thing she wanted most. Ann was certain that Dennis's second-mile offering would be to finally give her a priesthood blessing, and she wondered why it was taking him so long to figure that out. As she anxiously waited to see what Dennis would do, Ann had forgotten all about her own need for a healing miracle.

One day it occurred to Ann that she had never reassured Dennis that she would be grateful for *any* blessing he gave her. She realized that—as far as Dennis knew—as soon as he gave her this first blessing, all he would get from her would be a report card on how well he had done. Ann felt an apology growing in her heart.

Ann approached Dennis and told him that she understood that getting a revelation is no simple or automatic matter. Hadn't she seen that herself as she struggled in prayer to find out what had gone wrong between them? Ann told him that this was something they could grow in together, and if it took more than one blessing to really discern the Lord's will, then who was in such a hurry anyway? They could afford to practice together. The important thing was that they would someday be able to share this special and intimate part of their lives.

I hardly have to say that Dennis and Ann both realized the miracle they were seeking. What is further typical of such cases is that this crisis had no sooner passed than it seemed to shrink in importance. Having received each other again, they could no longer envision why anyone would ever choose to receive a fantasy of perfection while forfeiting the reality of an eternal companion.

CHRIST CAN RESTORE HEARTS

I've spent a lot of time talking about cases where the competing attraction is reasonably manageable. But what about those situations where the competing interest has grown into an addiction and the marriage is in serious jeopardy? Isn't it possible for a heart to grow so diseased that nothing can cure it?

Too often we think it's harder to perform a big miracle than it is to perform a little one. The fact is that any miracle is impossible without the Lord. Jesus taught that "if ye have faith as a grain of mustard seed, ye shall say unto this mountain, Remove hence to yonder place; and it shall remove; and nothing shall be impossible unto you" (Matthew 17:20). The Atonement was bigger than anything we can imagine, big enough to heal every wounded heart.

Rick and Denise

Rick married Denise in the temple without telling her about his lifelong homosexual inclinations. He had hoped that the ordinance alone would somehow change his desires. But that didn't happen, and early in his marriage, Rick had several brief encounters with men. Moreover, Rick had a recurring masturbation problem, usually accompanied by homosexual fantasies. Rick felt little peace in his heart and experienced little power in his Church callings, but he was a compassionate man, known for his willingness to help others. To outward appearances, Rick seemed to be the ideal husband, and Denise appreciated his cultural refinement and considerate nature.

Rick knew he should confess his sins to his bishop, and he even wondered if he should share his struggle with Denise, but he couldn't find the courage to do either of these things. He hoped God would be merciful, but he wasn't about to share his awful secret with anyone, least of all with someone who was close to him emotionally.

There came a day, however, when Rick felt he could no longer live a lie, and he confessed his sins in a worthiness interview. A disciplinary council soon followed, as he expected, but Rick was surprised at how supportive his priesthood brethren were. He sensed that many of them were determined to stand by him as he returned to full fellowship in the Church, and this became a great healing influence in his life.

For Rick, however, the seemingly insurmountable challenge was the council's injunction that he tell Denise about his problem. He couldn't tell which would be worse—to tell Denise that he had been untrue to her or to tell her that he had a competing attraction she could never compete with. Rick expected that Denise would be furious with him.

She was. But more than that, she was heartbroken. This revelation so shattered her world that Denise went through mourning for her marriage, and she prepared herself to live without Rick if that was his choice. But that wasn't his choice. Rick really did love Denise, even though he had never allowed himself the luxury of being honest with her. Rick felt sure that Denise could never receive the man he thought himself to be. He couldn't bear to reveal to Denise his innermost feelings, too ashamed of what she would see and certain she would leave him—yet the Spirit told him that this was precisely the offering he must make.

When Rick spoke to Denise the first time, he had confessed all his shameful deeds, and that had been hard enough to do. This time was far harder, as he told her about the thoughts and feelings behind those deeds. Denise listened quietly as Rick unfolded to her the other half of his life, and it was evident that she was trying to discern by the Spirit what she should say to him.

After he'd shared these feelings with her, I'll never forget how Denise reached over to Rick and turned him until he was facing her. She looked him in the eyes and told him that even though he had hurt her terribly, she could and would receive him as her eternal companion, both now and forever. They were both crying, but not from either sorrow or relief. Theirs were tears of conviction as they reestablished their commitment to their temple marriage. I recognized that both of them had made a significant second-mile offering.

Guardrail: Lose the Day After

While Rick's temptations didn't disappear overnight, they are no longer the ever-present challenge to him they once were. He has never again had encounters with men, and he quickly overcame his masturbation habit. Rick's second-mile offering reduced the strength of these temptations miraculously, and he found he could build guardrails to help him overcome smaller moments of temptation. His bishop suggested one important guardrail found in Leviticus 15:16: "And if any man's seed of copulation go out from him, then shall he wash all his flesh in water, and be unclean until the even."

Rick kneeled beside his bed and prayed aloud, covenanting that if he ever again masturbated, he would remain at home the following day, abstaining from all work, play, or entertainment until the sun went down, at which time he would shower and again reenter his normal life.

While at first this seemed to be getting off too easy, Rick soon found that this nonescalating consequence provided just enough punishment to be an effective deterrent. He found himself interrupting the temptation cycle with such thoughts as, "I don't believe I'll masturbate tonight. I have things I want to do tomorrow!"

Where before Rick might have simply shut his mind off and proceeded to indulge, now he found himself weighing the choices. He was thinking again.

In the morning, Rick would not feel the temporary insanity of the night before. Consequently, he began to measure success by how long he had kept his new covenant, rather than by how long it had been since he last indulged in masturbation. Rick found he was much more successful when his moral battles were reduced to this smaller scale.

Guardrail: Gift of Self

Moreover, Rick has found an even more effective guardrail to his homosexual feelings. He has learned that when he does feel the temptation begin to grow again, he can reduce it significantly by spending personal time with his wife, giving her the gift of himself. He now knows that nothing raises his stock in himself as much as being the man that Denise loves and needs. Whenever Rick feels like Denise's hero, he can't imagine ever having another homosexual thought. Rick may never altogether lose this weakness in mortality, but he has found that loving as Jesus loves leaves little room in his heart for any competing attraction.

But what do we do if the competing attraction is an ongoing affair? What if the unfaithful partner would like to save his marriage but doesn't want to lose his competing love? Is there anything he can do that will change his heart enough so he can make this decision and stick with it?

Carl and Susan

I once counseled a woman who was in this situation. Although Susan was sealed to Carl, she began a non-sexual office romance with her nonmember supervisor, Jim. There were several occasions when Susan and Jim agreed to end things between them, yet one or the other kept returning. Susan frankly worried more about how Jim was feeling than she did about Carl, but she didn't think about Carl's pain any more often than she had to.

I suggested that Susan's feelings for Carl might grow stronger if she were to make a second-mile offering, a sacrifice so profound that the Lord would surely touch her heart. Susan knew I was suggesting that she should end this emotional affair, whether or not she could salvage her marriage. She knew that burning that bridge would leave her alone if Carl left her, but she also knew that nothing less than that would work. She put off doing anything for a while longer.

About a month later, Susan telephoned me to say that she'd done what she knew she had to do. She brought Jim and Carl together and told both of them that she was going to be true to her temple sealing. She told Jim that she wanted to transfer to another department so she would never have anything to do with him again.

Susan took Carl's arm as she made this announcement, and she saw tears come to Jim's eyes. While it was difficult for her to watch Jim leave that day, Susan was sustained by the Spirit, and she had an increasing witness that she had done the right thing. Her relationship with Jim ended that day, and Susan and Carl are still together.

The hardest cases in marriage counseling are the ones in which one of the spouses awakens one morning and announces that his feelings have died, and the temple marriage is over. He usually adds that he will continue to provide materially at the same level as before so that family members will hardly notice the change. Although this can occur with couples who have experienced marital distress in the past, more often than not this represents the first time the departing spouse has ever expressed this level of dissatisfaction. Either way, the abandoned spouse is devastated by the news.

When clients have blandly announced, "My feelings have died," I used to think they were trying to provoke the other spouse to express love, make concessions, or at least beg for another chance. I have since discovered that there is usually no such underlying motive. Most typically, there is no one else or anything else competing for their attention. The relief of unloading emotional responsibility for others *is* the competing attraction. What makes these cases so difficult is that this feeling of relief anesthetizes their hearts, and where there is no pain, there is little desire to seek a healing miracle.

Tim and Nancy

I have seen a few cases, however, where marriages have survived this crisis. Tim and Nancy had seemed the ideal couple. Tim was a lifelong member of the Church and had held positions of responsibility at a younger age than most. Both his career and private life seemed satisfying to him. Then one day, Tim suddenly decided he was tired of doing the right thing all the time. He made the typical promises about providing for his children and then moved out of the family home.

Tim was very hesitant to come for counseling, fearing he'd be made to feel guilty and pressured to go home, but he finally made arrangements for an assessment interview. In the first session, he claimed he felt dissatisfied, not depressed. In fact, Tim felt fairly peaceful and happy when he could just be by himself or with people who didn't matter. He said he wanted Nancy and their children to realize they couldn't hold onto him as they wanted to. Tim didn't want to confront their issues; he wanted to run away. He felt an overpowering urge to escape family life, and he was afraid he'd be talked out of leaving.

But Tim also knew the Lord was displeased with his decision to leave. He agreed with me that it was his heart that had changed and that no one else could repair the damage. He would have to be the one to take the medicine. Tim had not forsaken his lifelong pattern of sincere daily prayer, and he felt prompted in prayer to make a second-mile offering. He felt the Lord telling him to sit down with Nancy and talk to her about what he was feeling.

It wasn't easy. Tim found himself turning the conversation to practical concerns, such as their son's braces and their daughter's dance recital. Then he realized he was only delaying his second-mile offering. He took a deep breath and told Nancy that he wanted her to understand what he was feeling. Tim told her he was afraid of failure, of coming in last in the race, and that he was tempted to change races.

Nancy was also afraid and more than a little angry as well. It wasn't easy for her to listen to Tim as he expressed his desire to be free of her, and she felt a great loss. Nancy was inspired, however, to tell Tim that she felt their old life together was over. If they were to have a future together, it would have to be a new beginning. She asked Tim what a new life together might be like, and—for the first time in several weeks—Tim was intrigued by the possibilities! It was frightening for Tim and Nancy to leave virtually all familiar ground, but during the days that they discussed their new options, they began to notice a calm spirit, reassuring them that it was going to be okay.

Before Tim made his second-mile offering, he had been willing to trade an eternal family for temporal freedom. When he reached out to talk with Nancy, however, Tim opened his spirit to the Savior's healing touch, and he experienced a change in his heart. The Lord inspired him to change his marriage, not throw it away. Tim and Nancy might have gone to friends for sympathy or to an attorney for legal advice, but instead they came to the Lord, and they were healed.

The plan of salvation has thrust upon us the responsibility for making choices, and there are many things that can entice us away from keeping our covenants. But none of those things is so big or so powerful as to render us helpless witnesses to the demise of our temple marriages. When we find ourselves putting something else first in our lives, be it duty, fantasy, sin, or freedom, we can set things straight again by making a second-mile offering to the Lord. Jesus Christ has the power to restore lost feelings to our hearts if we will but call upon Him for a healing miracle. He will keep His promises.

If a brother or sister be naked, and destitute of daily food,
and one of you say unto them, Depart in peace, be ye warmed
and filled; notwithstanding ye give them not those things
which are needful to the body; what doth it profit?

—James 2:15–16

CHAPTER SIX

BE YE WARMED
AND FILLED

It is believed that the James who wrote this epistle was Jesus'
half-brother, who would certainly have been an eyewitness to the
pure love of Christ. There must have been many times that James
watched as his older brother stepped forward to help the younger
children. But it's unlikely that their lives were just one miracle
after another. It doesn't seem that Jesus began to intervene miraculously until everyone was much older, after His first miracle at
the marriage in Cana (see John 2:11).

Until then, His acts of service to family members would
have been things that anyone could have done. However, those
acts of service were based on a love and a willingness to sacrifice

that only Jesus could show. And so we find James directing the Church: "But be ye doers of the word, and not hearers only. . . . Pure religion and undefiled before God and the Father is this, To visit the fatherless and widows in their affliction, and to keep himself unspotted from the world" (James 1:22–27).

James may very well have been fatherless as a boy, since we hear nothing more of Mary's husband after Jesus' twelfth birthday.

James learned that feeling love doesn't amount to much unless we show it to the ones we love. Just saying, "Depart in peace" means little more than "Good luck! I hope someone else actually meets your needs." If the one I love is cold and hungry, I should share my coat and my supper. That's going to demonstrate and confirm the love I feel for him. Anything less will only demonstrate how much I wish I loved him.

None of us is perfect, and we don't love everyone in the world equally. We are selective about who we love. We may have good feelings toward everyone, and we may wish everyone the best, but we reserve our love for a much smaller group. We save our best blessings for family members, friends, neighbors, coworkers, or ward members—the ones we know best.

First in our hearts among mortals should be the person we married for time and all eternity. So far, we have mainly discussed how to repair a temple marriage that has been damaged by fear, resentment, or competing attractions. Our present concern, however, will be with feeding a marriage, not doctoring one. What can I do that will show my eternal companion that I have truly received her with all my heart, and how can she let me know she has truly received me in return?

What is it that men and women want from each other? Is there one answer to this question? To say that women like expensive gifts and men like to be fed on time is often true, but a sizable percentage of couples would just shrug and say that those things are not important to them. To say that men use love to get sex and women use sex to get love is an oft-quoted (albeit somewhat cynical) truism, yet there are many couples who have those priorities reversed. Moreover, there are plenty of men and women who want both sex and love in their lives and who would not easily accept a forced choice.

Our understanding of what men and women want from each other changes over time. The American public has changed its ideal of a normal marriage even during my own lifetime. If we doubt this, we just need to watch very old television reruns, which feature wives asking permission of their husbands to leave the house, husbands apologizing to their wives for being in the same room as an attractive woman, and even husbands spanking their wives.

So we will not discuss how to be the ideal couple of this decade or the next. Such styles change over time, and our children will no doubt find our image of an ideal marriage quaint and boring. We must accept that there is only a general answer to the question of what men and women each want: They want to be received by one another.

CREATED MALE AND FEMALE

How do men and women receive each other? How does a couple reassure one another that the union they feel will never revert to *you* and *me* again? Do men and women do this in the same way? If a man treats his wife in a certain manner and she feels received by him, will the same treatment from her make him feel received? We tend to give our spouses what we wish they would give us, but is this always a good strategy?

Since what we are talking about is the gift of self to our spouses, then that gift is going to be the same if men and women share the same sense of self, and different if they do not. When I close my eyes and feel what it's like to exist, that experience is virtually identical to what my wife would feel if she were doing the same thing. But I believe the experience would be different in a few subtle ways.

Those ways in which they differ only emerge when we examine more closely how little girls are different from little boys. I know it's politically correct these days to assume that boys and girls only behave differently because we train them to be that way. That sounds great in theory, but anyone who has raised a family with both boys and girls knows better.

At one year of age, I expected much the same behavior from both my sons and my daughters—patty-cake and peek-a-boo play just about the same for boys and girls at that age. Granted, there were times that my daughters were aggressive and my sons were nurturing. Nevertheless, I can clearly recall times when there was no mistaking that the boys were boys and the girls were girls.

I remember one day when my wife was playing Roll the Ball across a long table with my toddler son. She had played this with my two older daughters, and it didn't take them long at all to catch on to rolling the ball back to her. However, I could see as I was walking through the room that my son was having problems with this activity. He would watch his mother roll the ball underhanded to him, and he would try to mimic what she had done. But it just didn't feel right to him. Suddenly, I saw his face light up with new comprehension as he reached back and tossed the ball overhanded and laughed to see it go over her shoulder. He made no further attempts at underhanded pitches but stayed with what worked for him.

I remember the day he first learned to walk. Like most children, he had been cruising around furniture for some time, and we were all waiting for him to make the leap to walking across the room. We had practiced with him by holding his hand as he walked a few steps and then encouraged him to step forward on his own. On this particular day, my wife was trying to take a picture of his first step, and my oldest daughter was the one who was working with him. My wife got the picture.

My son was, of course, happy to be more mobile, but what I most treasure about that picture is the expression on my daughter's face. Pure love. She wasn't working to gain anyone's approval by being motherly, and she wasn't rejoicing in the efforts of a little child because it was her feminine duty. That soft expression with just a hint of tears in her eyes said it all. We didn't train her to have those feelings; she was born that way.

And she's the athletic one. She wasn't half as prissy as her little sister. I tried my best to get that second daughter to be a little more assertive and a little less shy, but she didn't make those changes until she was good and ready to do so herself. If these children are so malleable that they become whatever their parents envision them to be, why don't parents do a better job of it?

Why was it that I had such trouble getting my daughters to settle down and stop giggling, while I had just as much trouble getting my sons to settle down and stop wrestling? How many times had I come into their bedrooms with a serious expression on my face and with what I believed was a convincing voice of command directing them to stop it now and clean up their room, only to hear the girls resume their giggling and the boys resume their wrestling before I had made it down the hall? Did we train the girls to giggle and the boys to wrestle? I think not. I believe they came already hardwired for gender differences.

I don't see that this hardwiring subsides much as we mature either. The day I met my wife, another girl and I drove her to a friend's apartment. When we walked her to the top of the stairs, we encountered a snarling Doberman pinscher who would have attacked us if he had not been restrained by a sturdy chain. We each operated by instinct: I faced the dog and put out my hands, while both girls stood behind me and pushed me toward the dog. After we realized we were going to live, we had a good laugh about it, but I think we were seeing something pretty basic about men and women. Of course, I'm sure that both girls would have stepped forward protectively if a child had been with them.

Men and women have more in common than they have differences, but their dissimilarities are real. Do the differences between men and women include their sense of self? I believe there's a fundamental difference in how men and women see themselves: Women define themselves first by what they *are*, while men define themselves first by what they *do*.

I've noticed that men get into big trouble when they try to define why they love their wives. No matter which reason he gives, she will often come back with "So, if I weren't doing that, then you wouldn't love me? Why don't you just hire someone who can do that?" If he says she's pretty, she wonders if he will still love her when she's older. If he says he respects how good she is in her employment, she wonders if he just likes her extra paycheck.

There seems to be only one acceptable answer, which is that he loves her because she is fundamental to his being. His life would be empty without her. If she died, she would carry a big part of him with her into the spirit world. He might remarry, but she could never be replaced in his old life; he would simply have to start building a new life. He loves her because of who she is, because knowing her, he can't help loving her.

On the other hand, I see women get into just as much trouble when they try to explain why they love their husbands. "I just can't help loving you" sounds suspiciously like "I love you *anyway*. I don't particularly like the way you do things, and I don't especially look up to you, and I'm not altogether proud of you—so I guess I love you the same way your mother does!" That isn't very comforting to most men.

He wants to hear precisely what it is he does that makes her want to associate herself with him so he can be sure and do it again. He wants to know there are some things he does that cause her to want to take his arm. He wants to know that she's proud of him when he speaks in sacrament meeting, that she likes knowing he can hold his own with other men on a work project, that she knows the children will pay attention when he tells them to do something, and that she feels confident that he will always provide for their family. He wants to call forth her loving feelings by the things he does.

Naturally, these are things that both men and women want, but I do think there's a difference in what they want *first*. Once she knows he cherishes her, then it also matters that he enjoys her competencies as well. Knowing she looks up to him, it's also nice to know that she won't stop loving him the first time he fails to measure up.

I've also noticed that when men and women hug each other, the man's arms are almost always on the outside. Even when the woman is taller than her husband, her arms are generally under his arms and around his waist, such that they both feel he is holding her. This is a comforting feeling for both of them. When the burdens of life seem too much for them, they can both feel comforted when he holds her this way. Occasionally, a man will feel so tired or discouraged that he lets his wife hold his head in her arms, but as soon as he feels a little better he'll almost always reverse their position.

This also emerges in their intimate life together. While I've certainly met women who seem to have a stronger sex drive than their husbands, I have never yet met a woman who doesn't prefer for her husband to initiate physical relations. She may follow an impulse to start things out, but she generally does so in hopes that he will take the wheel. Similarly, I've met men who either from fatigue, fear of rejection, or personal discouragement want their wives to initiate intimate relations, but as soon as things get underway, the men will often take the lead again. This tendency seems to be inborn, as common to middle-aged couples as to newlyweds and evident in different cultures around the world.

I see the same thing when it comes to taking the lead in other areas of life. When men and women walk together while holding hands, the back of the man's hand will almost always face the direction they are walking. Each couple clasps hands or intertwines fingers in their own unique way (I call this their signature clasp), but the man's arm is nearly always over her arm; hence, the back of his hand leads out.

This desire for the man to lead out seems nearly universal. The most common complaint I hear from Mormon wives is when their husbands won't take the lead in spiritual matters. If anyone is going to call the family to pray, she's the one who's got to do it. She's the one who reminds everyone that tomorrow is fast Sunday, the one who teaches the children to pray, and the one who suggests the priesthood blessing when one of the children is sick.

But she wishes her husband would take the lead in these areas. Of course, if she knows her husband is presiding, that he has assumed bottom-line responsibility for these things to happen in the home, she doesn't generally mind conducting. Ultimately, someone has to lead the family and, unless he has a punishing leadership style, everyone in the family wants the husband to be that someone.

On the other hand, there are equally challenging expectations that wives face in marriage. There is often an understanding that the wife is going to care as much about the needs of other family members as she does about her own needs. Everyone knows it's her job to keep the home running, even if she has a job outside of the home that takes as much of her time as her husband's job does. When her husband takes on tasks beyond his assigned chores, he sees himself as helping out, because the unwritten rule is that anything outside of his assigned responsibilities is her job. Any new task is automatically the wife's job unless someone deliberately adds it to the husband's list of assigned duties.

None of this is fair, and I know this unwritten rule is not politically correct, but this is the arrangement in almost every household. In the Church, we are taught that husbands should look for ways to assist their wives at home. Mormon women are proudest of husbands who wash dishes, fold clothes, and—especially—change diapers. In fact, the big heartedness to fully contribute as a parent is part of the Mormon definition of manhood. But that doesn't change the fact that these husbands are still helping out, stretching themselves to do some of what their wives automatically take on as their natural duty.

What's more, the husband's career typically defines the family's identity and social class. If the wife defers her own career until the children are raised, she has, in most cases, limited how far she can progress in that career. She is expected to hitch her wagon to her husband's star. This may relieve her of some performance pressure, but it also demands an incredible, and sometimes unappreciated, sacrifice of control in her life.

Her husband's occupation will likely determine the city they live in, the size of their home, the recreations they enjoy, their children's social circle, and how tightly she will have to budget their income to make ends meet. It takes much faith to marry a man who has not yet proven himself in his career. He may not have even chosen his career. That is the faith of every woman who enters a marriage, takes on her husband's surname, and begins to bring children into the world.

The flip side of that expectation is the understanding most couples have that it's the husband's responsibility to provide for the family's basic financial needs. Here it is the wife who is helping out, even if she makes more money than he does. If they get into a financial bind, everyone turns to the husband for a solution.

When I was a child, I recall thinking that my father was a hero for supporting our family. It is no longer stylish to idealize the breadwinner of the family, but the fact remains that married men take on a lifelong financial responsibility for their families. Men and women have different roles in a family, and both roles require faith and courage.

TO RECEIVE ONE ANOTHER

I observed earlier that women tend to define themselves first by who they are, while men tend to define themselves first by what they do. When a man is holding a woman, she is mostly being and he is mostly doing. For him to hold her is a wonderful gift, one so special that almost every woman at some time or another has said to her husband that she would be happy enough to be held without sex.

That's a very nice thing to say, since it implies that she would rather be held by her husband than by any other man and that she has received him by receiving his embrace. Of course, her husband rarely hears what she is saying; he gets lost somewhere at the "without sex" clause. Too often, he replies that if she feels that way, he will wait for her to initiate sexual relations—even if that takes forever!

Sometimes it does take forever. Many women experience sexual feelings only when their husbands reach out to them first. They are wonderfully responsive but feel virtually no anticipatory sexual appetite. They wait to feel hungry before initiating physical relations, and then both individuals become discouraged when the hunger never comes.

This common marital scene is tragic because neither of the partners can see what she was originally saying: She was feeling received by her husband, and she was willing to receive him in return. After I had encountered this exchange between spouses in literally dozens of marriages, I realized that there are two general rules that distinguish how men and women receive one another:

> 1. Women feel received by their husbands when their husbands reach out to hold them, especially at times when the wives feel least attractive physically and emotionally.
>
> 2. Men feel received by their wives when their wives receive their gifts, particularly when the husbands identify strongly with the gift they're offering.

Let's consider the women first. Part of the burden of a woman's sensitivity is that from time to time she's going to feel negative about life, generally starting with herself and then radiating outward to everything and everyone. It's unlikely at such times that she's going to be any more tolerant of her husband than she is of herself. Most of the time he'll want to give her lots of room, even to the point of retreating from her altogether.

That's the worst thing he can do. While she may well appreciate a moment alone to catch her breath—and there's nothing wrong with giving her a short period of solitude—it doesn't help for her to feel abandoned. The husband must understand that his wife quickly becomes imprisoned in an emotional whirlwind, and she can't easily get out without his help. How could she hope that her companion would like her at a time like that? But when he does come to her and holds her in his arms, then she feels genuinely received.

Bill and Sandra
Bill and Sandra were in counseling to deal with the chal-

lenge of parenting a difficult teenager, yet I could tell they had a basically sound temple marriage. We had met a number of times, and they were making headway in resolving their issues. Then, in one session, Sandra suddenly began to rehearse her grievances against Bill. Before we knew it, she was on a real resentment streak, bringing up a seemingly endless list of times when Bill had been selfish, inadequate, or mean to her. Sandra left him no chance for a rebuttal.

Bill was sitting somewhat behind her line of vision, and she was so intent on what she was telling me that Sandra couldn't see his face. Bill lifted up his hands slightly in a gesture that said, "How do I get out of here?" I don't think he resented the hateful and demeaning things she was saying. Bill seemed to know that Sandra wasn't expressing any deeply held or thoroughly thought-out opinions, and he could tell she probably wouldn't want to be quoted the next day. The truth was, Bill didn't want to clarify anything; he just wanted to leave the room and wait for Sandra to calm down before being with her again.

Sandra was so upset that she didn't see me silently mouth the words, "Hold her!" Bill looked at me with an expression of disbelief, but I gave a slight nod of encouragement to him. Then, with an *I hope you know what you're doing* attitude, Bill gingerly placed his hand on Sandra's shoulder. She jerked away from him and then glared at him for trying to shut her up. But Bill continued to draw Sandra into his arms, saying, "Please, let me hold you for a moment."

Bill's voice didn't sound very confident, but something in Sandra began to relax, and then she started to cry, burying her face in Bill's shoulder. She became absolutely his, curling into his embrace, and she said to him, "It's all I need; it's the only thing I've ever wanted from you!" Bill was looking at me in amazement and quietly asked me if I had known it would turn out that way. I replied, "No, Sandra might've slapped you. But it seemed like a worthwhile risk to me." I'm not certain he appreciated my humor, but I think Bill did learn something about receiving his wife.

So, what about husbands? What do I mean when I say that

men feel received by their wives when their wives receive their gifts, particularly when the men identify strongly with the gift they're offering? On the whole, men tend to be more action oriented than relationship oriented. Their hearts usually follow their hands. They have to work with something before they can learn to love it.

In fact, it's hard for a man not to love what he has worked for. If he gave up two years to serve a mission, he's going to love the Lord and the Lord's Church more than he would otherwise have done. If he places himself in danger during a war, he will likely be more patriotic afterward. If he creates a business, he will love that business as his own child. Men's hearts follow their hands.

And the products of a man's hands are his gifts, the fiber and the essence of his love. If he can't give his gifts to the one he loves, he's going to have trouble loving at all. That's how his heart works, and it's vitally important to him that his wife receives his gifts. He may grumble about it beforehand, but that doesn't change the nature of the gift. Anytime he does something special for his wife, she needs to realize that she's holding his heart in her hands. She receives him by letting him give to her.

David and Kathy

David and Kathy had been married several years, but David was having trouble deciding upon a career. He chose an occupation that wouldn't require much schooling so they could quickly pass the sacrifice years. But David had no interest in that career, and he failed courses, took semesters off, and finally changed majors.

Kathy was exasperated. Each wasted semester added to their debt load, although Kathy was frugal enough that this never became too frightening. Still, Kathy was tempted to get a job in her own field, certain that she could provide for their family until David worked out their future.

That was a good plan, except that Kathy felt the Lord warning her that this good plan would destroy her husband. David needed to lay the foundation of their home as a gift to her, and if

Kathy rejected that gift, she would be rejecting David at the same time. Furthermore, this would take all the joy out of David's final career; after all, what good is a life's work if you're only working for yourself and if your sweetheart can do just as well for herself without you?

David and Kathy both found part-time jobs, and together they barely earned enough to get by while David was in school. Then Kathy asked David to pick a major on the basis of his interest, rather than on the basis of expected income or years of college required. David was overwhelmed that Kathy cared so much for him that she was willing to delay her own dreams so he could reach his.

David selected a major that clearly asked more of him academically than he'd ever been able to handle before, and they settled down for the several years it would take David to reach his goal. To his own surprise, David did outstandingly well in his courses.

After graduation, he entered his chosen career. David found he could support his family on his income alone. More important, his love for Kathy grew dramatically, along with his sense that everything he was doing was for her. David's career was his gift to Kathy, and she had received his gift. By doing so, she received his heart as well.

One very special gift a man can give his wife is a priesthood blessing. My own wife has built a special place in my heart by how she's received my priesthood blessings over the years. She's always transcribed these blessings, taking a moment to write down what she can recall. It's humbling to know that she places these experiences nearly on a par with her own patriarchal blessing.

I was even more humbled a few years ago when I came home from work and encountered her typing an index to the Book of Larry. I'll admit I was a little anxious about the possibility that some later blessing might contradict one of the earlier ones, but we didn't find any contradictions. Through the years, my wife has created a book of blessings for each of our children as well. Her attitude toward these has caused my children to ask for their book before making significant decisions. My wife has received me as she has received my gift of giving priesthood blessings.

She also receives me by receiving my gift of righteous living. My wife has always been certain I would do the right thing as soon as I knew it was right. The more she believes in me, the more I *want* to do what is right. It thrills me to think she feels herself lucky to have me for a husband; it makes me want to live up to her picture of me. The fact is, when my wife receives my gift of righteousness as a precious thing, I realize how precious it really is! She has touched my heart by receiving my gift.

Of course, I want her to feel received as well. I've held her when she's been happy as well as when she's felt down, and I've learned there's more than one way to hold her. Not only can I physically hold her in my arms, but I can hold her in my thoughts by listening to the concerns of her heart. As often as we can, we go strolling together in the evening. These are the times that we give each other our full attention.

Guardrail: Strolling

Strolling can become a guardrail for couples who want to overcome communication problems in their marriage. We learned years ago that our house is not designed for communication. Rather, it seems to have been designed specifically to prevent us from ever communicating at all. In the kitchen, there is the refrigerator and the pantry, both of which contain items that drown out my wife's sweet voice. Just when she's ready to tell me about some new discovery that she's made in the scriptures, I hear this voice whisper, "Toast and jam." I still keep one ear open to her, but the other ear is waiting for that toaster to pop up. No, the kitchen was never designed for talking.

But then, neither is the bedroom, with its bed inviting me to either sleep or get romantic. The living room isn't much better with the stereo and bookshelf, but even that's better than the den with the television set. The children's rooms are full of talking, but there isn't an inch that's designed for marital discussions. And no room is safe if it has a telephone or a computer.

We learned a long time ago that if we want to communicate, we must leave the house and walk down the street. If the weather permits, we follow a large circle through our neighborhood. The long route allows us enough time to say whatever is on our minds. We made a rule for ourselves that we would never retrace our steps, and we always hold hands in our signature clasp. Holding hands in our signature clasp says I love you as no other way would. Holding hands gives us very nearly the same sense of comfort that holding each other does. And whenever we hold hands that way, we can achieve a shared gait that feels natural to both of us. It almost feels like being rocked.

When our children were young, strolling gave us the chance to talk together without the constant interruptions of exuberant little ones. We would wait at night until they were sound asleep, and then we limited our walks to circling the block a few times. The kids knew when we were strolling, and if one of the younger children awoke, he knew to go to his big sister's bed, and she would turn on her bedroom light. Within three minutes, we'd walk past the house again, and we'd know when we saw the light that we needed to attend to the child who'd gotten up. Apart from that, our only rule was for the children to ignore the doorbell and the telephone (we had an answering machine).

I've been admonished that we took a risk that one of the children might have gotten up to play with matches. This wasn't a problem for us because, once asleep, our children have always wanted to stay asleep. I can't recall a single instance where one of them has fallen asleep in the evening and then gotten up again to play. Our family has never been hurt but only blessed by our nightly walks.

You might notice that I call what we do strolling. I want to make sure no one thinks we're out exercising. There is nothing aerobic about what we do. Neither of us is out of breath because we want to save our breath for talking. We don't usually know what we're going to talk about in advance; we just say whatever bubbles up in our hearts as we stroll. We don't waste good communication time with a planning meeting either. If all we need to do is plan calendars and budgets, we can stay home and compete with the toaster.

Strolling can become a guardrail for couples who want to overcome communication problems in their marriage. Over the years, we came to know each other better during our strolls than in any other setting or activity. When we go strolling, we might walk silently for a few minutes, watching the stars that peek through the city skies and then find something in our hearts that needs to be said. We may talk about what life felt like today, or some new perspective that we're trying out. Sometimes we share thoughts that are less profound.

I call this the poetry of our hearts. It's like when I awake in the morning and urgently tell my wife about a dream I had, reaching deep within myself to get it straight and tell it correctly. I'm no sooner done than we both break into laughter at how silly or meaningless it was—but for some reason it had to be told. Such are often the things we share as we stroll.

Sometimes we catch ourselves trying to hold different conversations at once, but usually we'll wait our turn. That's one nice thing about the longer circuit we have now; we both know how much time we have left before we get home, so we can both get in what we want to say. And if we don't, we can still spend a few minutes in our backyard swing.

There are times when we don't feel particularly received by one another. Neither of us is on such a perpetual spiritual high, and we don't always treat each other as we should. But the bottom line is that we both know we are kin, forever related and increasingly accepting of each other's gifts and weaknesses.

As the years have gone by, I have many times received her by holding her, both literally and figuratively, and she has many times received me by receiving my gifts. We have received each other often enough and profoundly enough that our marriage has been warmed and filled.

Our temple sealing has begun to grow into an eternal marriage. Inspired by God, preserved by God, our marriage is teaching us to know God. It feels like a miracle.

Wherefore, my beloved brethren, if ye have not charity, ye are nothing, for charity never faileth. Wherefore, cleave unto charity, which is the greatest of all, for all things must fail—But charity is the pure love of Christ, and it endureth forever; and whoso is found possessed of it at the last day, it shall be well with him. Wherefore, my beloved brethren, pray unto the Father with all the energy of heart, that ye may be filled with this love, which he hath bestowed upon all who are true followers of his Son, Jesus Christ; that ye may become the sons of God; that when he shall appear we shall be like him, for we shall see him as he is; that we may have this hope; that we may be purified even as he is pure. Amen.

—Moroni 7:46–48

CHAPTER SEVEN
THE PURE LOVE OF CHRIST

After the Nephite's final battle, Moroni reviewed the sacred records he had received from his father, and he decided to include a few items on the plates before he buried them. The most important of these was the synopsis of the Jaredite record, the book of Ether. Then he added the two letters and other brief instructions that make up most of the book of Moroni.

He also included Mormon's conference address (Moroni 7), which treated the same source text Paul used in his faith, hope, and charity talk found in 1 Corinthians 13. In Mormon's version, we learn that charity is one of the gifts of the spirit; in fact, it is the greatest of all spiritual gifts. Charity *is* the pure love of

Christ—the love that Christ feels, the love that Christ offers us, the love that we can be filled with.

What can we do to be filled with the pure love of Christ? Mormon says we have to pray fervently to Heavenly Father, present ourselves as true followers of Jesus Christ, and ask for this gift. If we do so, we will gradually grow to be "like him," filled with this love that "endureth forever." Charity "rejoiceth in the truth" (v. 45), and we will find ourselves wanting to do the right things for the right reasons, approaching the sanctification that is required to enter into the kingdom of heaven.

What's more, a man or woman who is filled with this love will want to receive their eternal companion and will want the loved one to feel received. Sometimes our selfishness may suppress that desire, but charity "is kind" (v. 45) and can overcome such selfishness. Those who receive the gift of charity find that both doctoring their marriage and feeding their marriage become the natural expression of their hearts. It becomes their truest joy to bless their companion's life, recognizing and meeting their deepest needs as guided by the Holy Spirit.

As with every challenge we've discussed, obtaining the gift of charity is going to require a miracle. In the concluding chapter of the Book of Mormon, Moroni exhorted us to "come unto Christ, and lay hold upon every good gift" (Moroni 10:30). He noted that "all these gifts of which I have spoken, which are spiritual, never will be done away, even as long as the world shall stand, only according to the unbelief of the children of men" (v. 19). This is not some unobtainable ideal; Moroni expects each of us to ask the Lord to fill our hearts with this great love.

It sounds too simple, doesn't it? Perhaps we want the gospel to be complicated so that we can put off until tomorrow what we need to do today: We need to ask Heavenly Father for the gift of charity. It can't be any harder than asking for the other miracles we've spoken about. Asking for the power to feel true love shouldn't be more difficult than asking for the Lord to stand by us in times of personal trial, to soften our grieved hearts, or to strengthen us in turning away from competing attractions. Jesus taught that Heavenly Father wants us to ask for these things:

"Or what man is there of you, whom if his son ask bread, will he give him a stone? Or if he ask a fish, will he give him a serpent? If ye then, being evil, know how to give good gifts unto your children, how much more shall your Father which is in heaven give good things to them that ask him?" (Matthew 7:9–11).

A BROKEN HEART AND A CONTRITE SPIRIT

If we want miracles in our lives and we know that the Lord is inviting us to ask Him for these miracles, why is it we hesitate to ask for them? Perhaps it's because we must "ask with a sincere heart, with real intent, having faith in Christ" (as Moroni went on to say in Moroni 10:4). We don't yet feel sincere or faithful enough; we don't want it badly enough yet—so we wait for another day to ask for our miracle.

Furthermore, we can only receive the gift of charity if we are willing to pay the price. Before a heart can be reassembled, it must first be broken. The gifts of God change us only as we use them. We can avoid the pain if we leave the gift alone, and we may be tempted to do so. We can't be sincere in asking the Lord for the gift of charity without a firm intention to reach out to others, especially our spouses, after we receive the gift.

"For what doth it profit a man if a gift is bestowed upon him, and he receive not the gift? Behold, he rejoices not in that which is given unto him, neither rejoices in him who is the giver of the gift" (D&C 88:33).

Virtually every time in the scriptures when the Lord makes a promise, gives a commandment, or offers a blessing, He couples it with the injunction that we must *receive* what He has given us. That's where man's agency comes into the picture. Heavenly Father won't ever force any gift upon us; we have to reach out and receive it. In fact, built into the commandment to receive our spouses is the truth that our eternal mates are precious gifts from God.

So what must we do to prepare our hearts to receive the gift of charity? I believe we've answered that question several times.

We must make an appropriate offering at the Lord's altar.

Throughout the centuries, men and women have prepared themselves to seek God by offering sacrifices. When Adam, Noah, and Abraham wanted to approach the throne of God, they offered their livestock. I'm sure at some point, their neighbors must have thought that the sheep could have been put to better use than just burning up the mutton, but these prophets know that sacrifice precedes communion with God.

In modern times, we might misunderstand, thinking it was the lamb who was making the sacrifice. But it was the worshiper who was sacrificing his wealth and his food. If we were to burn up a car or incinerate tomorrow's dinner, we would certainly call it a sacrifice. We would have put our money where our mouth is; we would have become more sincere and faithful in the process, perhaps enough that we'd be prepared to ask for our miracle.

Sometimes we think the Lord's atonement ended the offering of sacrifices, but this isn't the case. His atonement only changed the nature of the sacrifices we are to offer. The direction to offer sacrifices remains in full force.

Nowhere in the scriptures is this more plain than in 3 Nephi, chapter 9. Great destructions had come upon the inhabitants of the Western Hemisphere, and the survivors were anxiously enduring three days of pitch darkness. They couldn't see one another, but they could hear each other in the blackness, crying out in fear and remorse. Suddenly, a voice was heard "among all the inhabitants of the earth, upon all the face of this land." Each individual in his darkest hour heard the voice of Jesus Christ offering a new covenant to His people:

"O all ye that are spared because ye were more righteous than they, will ye not now return unto me, and repent of your sins, and be converted, that I may heal you? . . . Behold, I am Jesus Christ the Son of God. I created the heavens and the earth, and all things that in them are. . . . And ye shall offer up unto me no more the shedding of blood; yea, your sacrifices and your burnt offerings shall be done away, for I will accept none of your sacrifices and your burnt offerings. And ye shall offer for a sacrifice unto me a broken heart and a contrite spirit. And whoso cometh unto me with a broken heart and a contrite spirit, him will I baptize with fire and with the Holy Ghost" (3 Nephi 9:13, 15, 19–20).

Within two years after this remarkable experience, every single soul had converted to the gospel! "The people were all converted to the Lord, upon all the face of the land, both Nephites and Lamanites" (4 Nephi 1:2).

They must have joyfully received the missionaries sent forth by the resurrected Savior. I imagine the door approach was a simple declaration: "We were sent to you by *the voice in the dark*." Surely there was one question on everyone's lips: "What is the broken heart and contrite spirit? Jesus promised to heal me if I would bring him a broken heart and a contrite spirit. Did the Lord teach about that when He visited you?" And they must have received joyfully the message of all the Lord taught in His sermon on Mount Bountiful.

It's usually in our own darkest hour that the still, small voice of the Holy Ghost offers each of us this same promise of healing. All we must do in return is to offer up a broken heart and a contrite spirit. But what is a broken heart and a contrite spirit? When we say *brokenhearted*, we usually mean seriously disappointed, and *contrite* means something like repentant.

Was the Savior telling the Nephites they needed to be so let down by circumstances that they would finally repent? I don't think He was saying this. I think He meant that we have to bend our will to His until our pride breaks. He wasn't giving us an easier law after all. Now we don't just burn our food, we burn our pride. This is the price we must pay for a healing miracle.

It's a bargain at any price. It's little more than a token from us. The real price for each healing miracle was paid by Jesus Christ in Gethsemane, a price infinitely more expensive than any of us could afford. But even this bargain discount is beyond our means; even a broken heart and a contrite spirit are out of reach until He stands by us to help. However, if we no more than want to make our sacrifice, He will strengthen us to do so.

117

The Holy Ghost will help us define the second-mile offering that will break our pride. It will often consist in facing up to a fear, giving an enemy an undeserved break, or stretching past selfishness.

Guardrail: True Blessing

Occasionally we'll be inspired to bless another with what they've asked for or with what we think they deserve, but much more often we're inspired to bless another with what the Lord knows they really need. That's not an easy distinction to make, and it underscores why revelation is so essential to the process. In fact, one of the first guardrails I teach my clients is to ask Heavenly Father to show them what they can do (perhaps what *only they* can do) that would truly bless another person's life.

Even non-Christians sense the need to open communication with heaven by making a sacrifice. This doctrine is basic to virtually all of the world's religions. Regardless of how we envision God, we may all sense the inner wisdom that tells us which sacrifice God expects us to make.

But Satan has an effective strategy to defeat this impulse. He focuses our attention on what is fair or reasonable, and suddenly the whole idea of making an offering seems quite foolish.

Only Christianity has an answer to this objection, because it is the doctrine of the Atonement that balances justice and mercy. My small second-mile offering is a very modest price for a healing miracle. The offering that Jesus made for me in Gethsemane was more costly than I can ever imagine. The Atonement declares those two offerings a fair exchange.

My spirit can sense that the two sacrifices are somehow connected. When I make a second-mile offering, I almost physically feel the effect on my heart. The Atonement gives me my only chance to claim the healing miracles that lead to personal salvation. Without such miracles, I could never hope to keep my covenants nor hope to realize the covenant blessings. Without Christ's atonement, how could I possibly obtain what the temple sealing covenant promises?

THE MULTITUDE OF PROMISES

Did the Nephites know about temple marriage? They held the Melchizedek Priesthood and they built temples, so we can assume they performed Melchizedek Priesthood ordinances in those temples. But where in the Book of Mormon does it actually say they did?

One of the most thrilling verses to me has been 4 Nephi 1:11, which says, "And they were married and given in marriage, and were blessed according to the multitude of the promises which the Lord had made unto them." This verse describes one of the changes in Nephite society following the Savior's visit. They developed a cooperative economy, rebuilt cities, worshiped in a new way and ended war and racism—and there was some change in what marriage meant to them! When did Jesus make these promises? What were the promises He made?

We have a detailed account of what Jesus taught the Nephites during the first two days of His visit to them, but the third day's lessons were top secret and were not given to us.

"And it came to pass that he did teach and minister unto the children of the multitude of whom hath been spoken, and he did loose their tongues, and they did speak unto their fathers great and marvelous things, even greater than he had revealed unto the people; and he loosed their tongues that they could utter. . . . Behold, it came to pass on the morrow that the multitude gathered themselves together, and they both saw and heard these children; yea, even babes did open their mouths and utter marvelous things; and the things which they did utter were forbidden that there should not any man write them" (3 Nephi 26:14, 16).

Jesus held a separate session for the little children on his first two days in the Americas. On the third day, the little children gave the talks. What doctrines did they teach their fathers? These truths were "even greater than he had revealed unto the people," so sacred that no one could write down those doctrines. Note that these doctrines were not just too difficult to put into words; they were forbidden to be written!

Which doctrines today are too sacred to publish? Does it not seem reasonable that on the third day of conference, the little children taught their parents about eternal marriage and the sealing of families? Might these not have been the "multitude of the promises" that governed Nephite marriages after the Savior's visit? Who could touch the parents' hearts better than their little ones?

If this is true, then we also have a multitude of promises because we've been taught the same doctrines, and we have the same ordinances in our dispensation. There is a power that comes by keeping our temple covenants that can transform our lives from hopeless to livable, and from mediocre to glorious.

Raul and Marta

I've noticed that every ward has one special family that provides a little mission home for the full-time missionaries. In my mission, it was Raul and Marta's family. If we were tracting in their neighborhood, we'd always stop by for a few minutes. They didn't crowd about us as nearly everyone else did. They'd invite us into their living room, lower the lights, put on soft music, and then leave us alone for fifteen minutes or so. That home was such a refuge from the storm for us, a temple in the midst of the desert! We didn't take it for granted, and I don't recall that we abused the privilege, but just visiting their home and feeling the sweetness of their spirit would rejuvenate us—and we would soon be on our way again.

The last Sunday I was in that area, Marta invited us to dinner. As we sat at the table, my companion began to discuss one of our investigating families and how the husband in that home would have to work hard to overcome his Word of Wisdom problems. Raul looked up from his meal and commented that he himself had struggled with such problems before his baptism. I smiled. Surely Raul's sins had been small and long ago.

Then their seven-year-old daughter, Juanita, got up from her chair and walked to where Raul was seated. She climbed up in his lap, hugged his neck, and said, "Yes, that was in the days that Daddy beat us." I thought she was kidding, but Marta said, "There were times we had to flee to the shelter, and I might have divorced Raul then, except he was so ill from his chronic drunkenness that I expected him to die first." All the children nodded their heads silently as they recalled those days.

I couldn't believe what I was hearing! The ones I looked to as my example of the perfect family had gone through such hell only four years earlier! If it was true, then they'd only been sealed as a family within the last two or three years. Had Raul really beaten his little girl? If he had, how could Juanita snuggle up in his arms now and feel such love for him? What miracle had happened in this home to account for the spirit of peace that filled this family?

We learned that Marta and the older children were baptized first and that it was several years later that Raul experienced his personal conversion and was baptized. Several humble men in the ward befriended him, and the more he felt the Spirit, the less tempted he was to drink. His confidence grew, and he eventually petitioned to take out his own endowments. He held callings of increasing responsibility, and his self-image changed. He no longer identified himself as a recovering alcoholic; increasingly he saw himself as an elder in the Church.

Finally, Raul asked Marta and the children if they could ever forgive him enough to be sealed to him. Filled with the spirit of restitution, Raul did everything he could think of to make it up to them, continually praying that the scars might somehow go away. Now, just a few years later, I felt a home full of the pure love of Christ.

Raul and Marta had progressed from baptism to endowment and from endowment to temple marriage. Their hearts changed as they kept their covenants. Moreover, their children received like blessings by inheritance. Their hearts were also healed so they could forgive their daddy and trust him again. Raul and Marta had broken an intergenerational chain of dysfunctional family life. Their children wouldn't have to repeat that pain. Indeed, there are a "multitude of the promises" for those who keep their covenants!

HIS HEALING TOUCH IN GETHSEMANE

That isn't to say, of course, that eternal marriages don't have challenges or problems. I don't expect that after keeping my baptismal, endowment, and sealing covenants, I'll never again have weaknesses, face adversity and misfortune, or fight any weeds in my garden of life. In fact, there's good reason to believe that life gets more serious the closer we come to the light. We recall the "comforting" words that Joseph Smith received in Liberty Jail, "If the very jaws of hell shall gape open the mouth wide after thee, know thou, my son, that all these things shall give thee experience, and shall be for thy good" (D&C 122:7).

The most bone-chilling question I've ever encountered is if Heavenly Father really loves all His children, then *tell me why* He would send some of His own little children into awful homes where they will be mistreated, abused, taught to sin, and driven to hate those nearest to them? Oh, I wish I had the answer to that question! I wish I were wise enough to explain how those little children are going to be better off in the long run than they would have been with parents who would love and care for them.

There seems to be pain enough to spare for all of us in this period of time we call mortality. Most of us are going to experience intense physical pain, discouraging opposition, or mental or emotional disabilities. Even in the most blessed of lives, there will be moments so painful that we might wish for an early release. Sooner or later, all of us are going to ask, "What is the meaning of this pain? How is this helping anyone?"

I don't have all the answers for my own pain, let alone for everyone else's. But I've noticed that the sufferer is the only one who can hope for an answer to these questions. Those who love him enough to suffer with him may find that they are more challenged by these questions than he is. For example, at the time of Joseph Smith's leg operation, his mother couldn't endure to see what he was going through and had to leave the room. Yet Joseph was somehow able to endure until it was over.

What are the answers to these questions? What do the survivors of such adversity tell us after the storm is over? The answers don't come in carefully defined words that explain why it wasn't so bad after all. The answer I generally hear is simply, "It's okay," which doesn't answer the question for anyone else at all. The important thing is that it seems to answer the question for the sufferer, at least partially so. I have also experienced some painful moments in my life, when "It's okay" seemed to sum up something that had been placed in my heart.

The doctrine that makes sense of it all is the Atonement. Jesus actually experienced my pain, my shame, my guilt, my illness, my weakness, my temptation, and even my mortality. Each time I suffer those things I meet Him in Gethsemane. I hold onto the fence tightly and do everything I can to resist going there, but sooner or later I will be dragged to Gethsemane—and only then and only there will I receive the Savior's healing touch.

What is the meaning of my pain? There is no meaning at all in any of it—until I receive healing from the Lord. There is no meaning in any part of my life, neither pain nor pleasure, until I find God and obtain a healing miracle. We hear much today about the walking wounded, but I believe all of us are wounded—by the Fall if by nothing else. Each of us is going to require healing miracles from the Lord, and the greatest of these is the Resurrection. And that is the meaning of it all!

The question of questions is not "What is the meaning of pain?" but rather "Is there meaning in anything except pain?" Peace and pleasure are nice, and I do my best to find all the peace and pleasure I can, but I can't say that I find them particularly meaningful. Somehow it seems that my summer vacations have just served to separate my school years. When I look inside to see what I'm made of, it seems that most of me was constructed during the hard times.

On the other hand, I also feel that life has meaning when I'm blessed by the power and presence of God. I feel meaning during prayers, priesthood blessings, sacrament meetings, and in the temple. Our sacrifices give us joy in our blessings as well as comfort in our afflictions. Side by side with the tree of knowledge is the tree of life, and we find needful fruit on both trees. The painful fruit of the tree of knowledge brings our hearts to say, "It's okay," while the joyful fruit of the tree of life causes our hearts to sing, "It is good." And both fruits inspire our hearts to seek the gift of charity.

WE CAN GO THERE TOGETHER

At the heart of our religion is the new and everlasting covenant we have with the Lord. If we will meet Him in Gethsemane, He will give us the joy of His presence and the healing miracles we require. These are the experiences that give meaning to our lives.

Moreover, when I receive my eternal companion in that new and everlasting covenant, she and I will be able to share those experiences together. It will be our life together that becomes meaningful. I will find meaning in my wife's joy and pain as well as my own. When she goes to meet the Savior in Gethsemane, I'll be going there with her. As one flesh, having received each other in our temple sealing, we are going to make that trip together. This is good; I don't like making that trip alone.

I did make that trip alone for a long time, though, even several years after our temple marriage. Our life together was filled with laughter and tears and much love—yet our sincerest prayers were still too private and personal to share with anyone. We found we could pray together about anything at all, except when we were praying for the Savior's healing touch. Neither of us was prepared to uncover our wounds to the other in preparation for the journey to Gethsemane.

In retrospect, I believe we might have had some of our more unnecessary disagreements simply as distractions, smokescreens enabling us to meet the Savior without detection.

Years ago, when we were first learning about healing miracles, my wife and I would discuss our thoughts and feelings during our evening strolls. We shared with each other our fears, resentments, temptations, and disappointments. But we could only talk about these things after we had individually found relief in the Savior's touch. If we tried to discuss them before doing this, there would be misunderstandings and hurt feelings. We could count on it.

I will never forget one morning when we'd had some petty disagreement. I concluded with a guilt bullet, sarcastically thanking her for starting my work day off in such a fashion. It worked; she was stung into silence, and I left having gotten in the last word. But just as I closed the door, she said, "Wait, here's your lunch," and she carried it across the room to me.

It seemed to me that my wife had won. She had figured out a way to conclude our spat with her looking better than me, and I wished I had remembered the lunch myself. I felt foolishly indebted to her, and I wanted to say, "Thanks, but don't think this is going to make up for what you said to me this morning!"

And then I realized what she had done. My countenance softened, and I asked her, "Did you just make a second-mile offering to the Lord? That wasn't for me, was it?" It was immediately evident by her face that I was right, but she replied, "I really don't want to talk about it." We didn't say anymore about it then, but we did talk about it later, and it was the very first time that we really knew each other without the veil between us.

Since then, we have sometimes been able to share the experience of making our sacrifice to the Lord. We have prayed together for the strength to make a second-mile offering, and when one of us has blessed an enemy with an unearned gift, the other one has added something to that offering as well. If one heart is wounded, both hearts are wounded, and we must both bring a sacrifice to the Lord's altar. When we've been able to do this, we've shared both the pain of the wound and the joy of the healing. We've felt the Savior holding us as we hold each other.

Perhaps our greatest trial was the decision by one of our adult children to turn away from the gospel. In our pain, we felt the temptation to pull away from him and even to draw apart from each other. We alternated between the hope that this was simply part of the normal adolescent individuation process and the fear that with the passage of time he would lose even the light and testimony he once had. He seemed intent on proving he could succeed in life without any help from the Lord, and we anguished with him as he fell short on many of his goals. He just couldn't see that covenant children only prosper as they come unto the Lord.

But then we both felt inspired to pay his expensive out-of-state tuition so he could return to college. This came at a time when we couldn't really afford it, and it represented considerably more investment than we had made in the education of our other children. We knew it was more of a bailout than a treat, but we also knew our hearts had to be healed before we could think about anything else. We had to turn the other cheek first; then the Lord could lead us in reaching our son. We knew the Lord wanted us to make this second-mile offering together.

The Lord blessed us almost immediately. Our son soon began to open his heart to us, sharing both his dreams and disappointments. We also began to receive the same sort of material blessings often reported by parents of missionaries, such that we could not only afford to help this son, but we could also provide more assistance to our other three grown children. Most important, however, we drew together in a special way. We felt we were on the same team as we pleaded with the Lord for our son's soul. We felt one with each other again.

We have truly received a "multitude of the promises" as we've made our offerings to the Savior, but the most vital of all these promises has been the renewal of our own hearts. We've knelt together at the Lord's altar, our own will bending and our pride breaking as we made a second-mile offering, but our pain has been swallowed up in joy as the Lord has touched our hearts to heal them.

We've personally experienced the relief that comes as we lay down our burden of fear, or resentment, or temptation, and we remember our pains no more. We've felt the gift of charity fill our hearts with a desire to bless each other with more than what was asked for—far more than what was deserved, but what was truly needed. We've experienced the removal of the beam from our eyes so we could see clearly how to meet those needs. Our hearts have changed so that our deepest joy is in making each other happy. More and more often now, we find ourselves on the same side of the veil.

This is most sacred, the core of our beings, our own Holy of Holies. We're not there yet, but our temple sealing covenant has put us on the path that leads to eternal marriage, and even eternal life. This is the pure love of Christ, and we become most like Jesus when we obtain the gift of charity and use that gift to receive each other in the new and everlasting covenant of marriage.

Doing so will bring us the most joy and comfort that life has to offer now and will prepare us to receive the highest degree of glory in the life to come. It is the surest and straightest road leading us back to our first home, the home where we first witnessed an eternal marriage.

REVIEW OF THE GUARDRAILS

1. SIX-SHOOTERS

The first step in reducing painful marital communications is to identify shaming or guilt-invoking statements. Naturally, we are more alert to our own pain than the pain of others—so we first identify statements that cause *us* distress. If we felt put down, demeaned, ignored, or dismissed—if the other person sees us as weak, ineffectual, stupid, or childish—then we've just been shot with a shame bullet. If we feel blamed, accused, resented, or challenged—if the other person sees us as powerful, mean, smug, or parent-like—then we've just been shot with a guilt bullet. Once we get pretty good at identifying which bullet has just struck us, we may then move on to recognize when we are shooting back—and which pistol we are firing. Since we all have agency, we can choose to put both pistols back in their holsters and raise our hands to either side in a gesture of peace. The battle winds down quickly once one of the participants stops returning fire, and we can eventually learn how to stop a word fight before it begins.

2. LEVELS OF CONFLICT

a. *Discussion*—It doesn't matter if we agree or not. The topic is neither important nor personal enough to fight over.

b. *Disagreement*—Each feels he's right, but neither loses his temper. Both can wait until the other finally sees they're right.

c. *Argument*—Each feels he's right, and tempers begin to rise. Each becomes frustrated that the other can't or won't understand.

d. *Quarrel*—The focus shifts to what's wrong with each other. They defend themselves to the death and don't want to be quoted.

e. *Shutdown*—Someone says or does something to end this *now!* It can be a slammed door, a slap, a threat, or other last word.

f. *Disengagement*—One or both no longer feels like trying. The tension vanishes when they are apart, and they're investing elsewhere.

3. TIME-OUT WALK

Couples can interrupt the escalation of conflict between them. The first one to recognize that he or she is approaching the quarrel stage should make the T sign for time-out, and then say the magic words: "I'm going to take a quick walk. I'll be back in five minutes, *and then we'll try again!*" When he or she returns, they'll try to discuss the same topic again as promised. If tension again rises, it will be the other person's turn to say the magic words and take the walk. Continue until one of you gets tired of walking and finds another way to calm down. This guardrail addresses the concerns of both the *Walker* and the *Talker.* The Walker firmly believes that the whole thing will blow over if they just let it lie for awhile, and the Talker firmly believes that they should talk it out once and for all, so they won't have to fight the same battle over and over. Both philosophies seem equally justified, and that's why it's essential that they actually *say* the magic words. The Walker gets to go off and calm down, while the Talker knows they'll return to their discussion in short order.

4. Sign-off Book

Polarized couples can see each other clearly enough to discern where their differing opinions have become grossly exaggerated. After they identify an area where they see themselves as *opposites,* they obtain a spiral notebook and commit to making only joint decisions for a week or two. Before either of them can implement any decision in that area of life, they must first discuss and agree on that decision. They must write down the decision, and both must sign off on it. If for any reason they are unable to discuss the matter, then the one forced into a unilateral decision must make the decision he or she truly believes the other spouse would make—and write that decision down and sign off on it. When they are together again, the other spouse can review the decision and give feedback on how well his partner was reading him—and sign off on the decision if he agrees with it. In most cases, the spouse making the original guess will realize that they are *different* from each other but not *opposites* after all—and both are within the normal range.

5. Gift to the Lord

Resentful couples can overcome their internal resistance to blessing each other by reframing their second-mile offering as a gift to the Lord instead of a concession to their spouse. They should make their offer to the Lord in private prayer beforehand and return and report to the Lord afterward. It's even more effective when the other spouse doesn't even know about the gift, because then the one offering the gift isn't as likely to measure success by any change in how their partner treats them in return. Rather, success is measured by a change in the heart of the gift-giver.

6. True Blessing

We can often identify the correct second-mile offering by first identifying our *enemy* (Who has robbed me of my inner peace?) and then determining what the Lord would have us do to bless that individual. We should recognize and avoid the tendency to either give in (granting that person what they're asking for) or punish (give that person what they deserve or what they've earned). Rather, we should seek inspiration to see that person through the Lord's eyes and identify the blessing that would promote *joy* in that person's life—usually something that might inspire him to follow his better self.

7. Treats, Not Bailouts

Couples with one responsible party and one irresponsible party can reduce the tendency for the one to take over for the other. The responsible spouse must first recognize how she feels the painful consequences of letting the ball drop more than the other spouse does—and how that prevents the irresponsible spouse from learning from his own pain. Whenever one person in a dyad takes the job of worrying, the other person invariably relaxes. The responsible spouse must resist the urge to fix things one last time (another bailout). Instead, she must take this energy and put it into a treat, some act that will show how much she loves him, yet doesn't interfere with his experiencing the consequences of his own decisions. Most people learn quickly from their own pain. Very few people learn from the pain of others.

8. Lose the Day After

If one spouse has a recurring bad habit (not a serious sin) that he or she just can't quite shake forever, that person should pray: "Lord, I haven't always been able to keep my first promise to Thee, that I would never do that misbehavior again, because

I don't always think straight when I experience temptation. But now I'll make a second promise that I *can* always keep, because I'll be keeping it when I experience remorse: I promise to follow up on my misbehavior by going apart from my daily life, and I'll do virtually *nothing* until the sun goes down, and then I'll shower and reenter life again." Those who truly believe in God and truly wish to keep their promises to Him—and who are determined to keep the second promise come what may—will find that their brains kick back into gear just prior to indulging. They'll begin to think about whether they really want to pay the price for indulging, and the act of thinking alone breaks the spell. Those who have followed this plan find that lapses are rare, and relapses are virtually nonexistent.

9. GIFT OF SELF

If one spouse is overly distracted by another person or activity but he wants to recapture his feelings of love for his partner, he should lose himself in *her* world. He should give her the gift of his time, his attention, and his self-disclosure. He should make the effort to *put into words* how he thinks and feels and also put into words his understanding of how she thinks and feels. It won't work if he's only waiting for her to overwhelm him with her thoughtfulness; he's got to be the one to win her back again. He should express to the world—preferably within earshot of her competitor—how much he cares for her and of his desire to put her first. He will honor her in every way he can think of. If he does this as a gift to the Lord, he will probably discover that his words and actions are not mere playacting but will become reality in his heart.

10. STROLLING

Couples who want to communicate better should regularly take walks along a predictable path, always holding hands in their signature clasp, and settling into a shared gait that feels natural to both of them. They should avoid making decisions or discussing sensitive subjects, but rather spend their time together discussing the simple thoughts that come to their minds. If one partner is usually silent, the other spouse might consciously drift off into silence at about the half-way point, and the quiet one will almost always begin talking soon thereafter. It's not unusual for both of them to see strolling as a drudgery *beforehand,* and perhaps they'll leave their home out of duty alone—but almost always they'll be glad upon their return that they shared this time together. Most couples find this side-by-side communication to be more natural and less threatening than staring at each other eyeball-to-eyeball.

About the Author

Larry W. Lewis was born and raised in Houston, Texas. He was in his first year of college at the University of Texas in 1969 when he had a religious experience that led him (and eventually eleven friends) to join the Church. Larry served a Spanish-speaking mission in Southern California from 1971 to 1973. He has enjoyed many callings in the Church, including early-morning seminary teacher, high councilor, and bishop.

Larry earned a master's degree in psychology from Stephen F. Austin State University in 1977, and he has worked for LDS Family Services since 1979. He has served as an area coordinator for the Association of Mormon Counselors and Psychotherapists

(AMCAP) in both Texas and North Carolina, and he has served as an area supervisor for AMCAP in Europe and the eastern United States. Larry is a licensed professional counselor and the clinical supervisor for the Farmington Agency of LDS Family Services.

Larry married Kendell Stout in the Manti Utah Temple in 1974, and they raised their four children while living in Spring, Texas; and Charlotte, North Carolina. They made temple attendance a priority from the beginning of their marriage, attending the temple once a year even during the early years of their marriage, when doing so necessitated a thirty-hour, nonstop car trip each way. Larry and Kendell reside in Layton, Utah, where they enjoy the privilege of living within a half-hour drive of three temples.